MUCH ADO ABOUT NOTHING

Edited by

ANNA KAMARALLI

Bloomsbury Arden Shakespeare
An imprint of Bloomsbury Publishing Plc

B L O O M S B U R Y
LONDON · OXFORD · NEW YORK · NEW DELHI · SYDNEY

Bloomsbury Arden Shakespeare

An imprint of Bloomsbury Publishing Plc

Imprint previously known as Arden Shakespeare

50 Bedford Square	1385 Broadway
London	New York
WC1B 3DP	NY 10018
UK	USA

www.bloomsbury.com

BLOOMSBURY, THE ARDEN SHAKESPEARE and the Diana logo are trademarks of Bloomsbury Publishing Plc

First published 2018

Editorial matter and selection © Anna Kamaralli, 2018

Text is taken from *Much Ado About Nothing*, Arden Shakespeare Third Series, edited by Claire McEachern, © 2006

Anna Kamaralli has asserted her right under the Copyright, Designs and Patents Act, 1988, to be identified as author of this work.

British Library Cataloguing-in-Publication Data

A catalogue record for this book is available from the British Library.

ISBN:	PB:	978-1-4742-7209-4
	ePDF:	978-1-4742-7211-7
	eBook:	978-1-4742-7210-0

Library of Congress Cataloging-in-Publication Data

Names: Shakespeare, William, 1564–1616 author. | Kamaralli, Anna editor.
Title: Much ado about nothing / edited by Anna Kamarilli.
Description: London : New York : Bloomsbury Arden Shakespeare, 2017. |
Series: Arden performance editions
Identifiers: LCCN 2017032179| ISBN 978-1-4742-7209-4 (pb) | ISBN 978-1-4742-7210-0 (epub)
Subjects: LCSH: Courtship—Italy—Messina—Drama. | Conspiracies—Drama.
Classification: LCC PR2828.A2 K35 2017 | DDC 822.3/3—dc23 LC record available at https://lccn.loc.gov/2017032179

Series: Arden Performance Editions

Cover design by Irene Martinez Costa

Series design by Terry Woodley

Cover images © Ashley Franklin and Sandra Cunningham/Trevillion Images

Typeset by RefineCatch Limited, Bungay, Suffolk
Printed and bound in Great Britain

To find out more about our authors and books visit www.bloomsbury.com. Here you will find extracts, author interviews, details of forthcoming events and the option to sign up for our newsletters

This book is for Innes Wilson, who makes all things possible.

CONTENTS

PREFACE

The impulse for the Arden Performance Editions came from a shared interest in creating an edition of Shakespeare that would best serve actors in a rehearsal room and also students in the classroom seeking to bring the text from page to stage. We wanted to provide a reliable text of each play, drawn from the scrupulously-prepared Arden Third Series editions and thus informed by the latest textual and historical scholarship, but newly thought-through, reannotated and redesigned with the practical needs of theatre-makers in mind.

This was partly about convenience – in terms of weight, print size, placement of notes, and concision of glossing. It was also about empowering actors and readers by making easily visible the sorts of editorial choices about lineation, punctuation and textual variants that can be less easy to discern in more lavishly-edited scholarly editions. We wanted to provide a clear sense of the available choices in terms of viable textual variants (where differing versions of a play survive from Shakespeare's own time), without getting embroiled in generations-old academic debates about whose emendations to which Elizabethan printer make the most sense. We also wanted it to be easy for our actor-readers to identify cases of ambiguous lineation, where different later editors have chosen to divide Shakespeare's verse-lines at different places: these editorial choices can prove misleading to an actor looking for certain 'clues' to delivery in the structure of the verse.

The punctuation of these editions was a matter of debate. We began by thinking that we might remove some of the bulky punctuation included in most modern editions, stripping it back to something more akin to that of some of the editions published in Shakespeare's lifetime – sparse punctuation that is often perceived as more 'actor-friendly'. However, it soon became clear that this was going to be difficult to implement across the board. Whilst we could have punctuated *Hamlet* based on the relatively sparse punctuation of the second quarto (1604), the same could not have been said of *The Tempest*, where the only extant early printed text is the heavily punctuated First Folio (1623). Here any choice of a minimal 'Elizabethan-style' revision to the punctuation would have been merely arbitrary, and would in many places have made Shakespeare's meaning less easy to discern rather than more so. In practice we have settled for the punctuation of the Arden Third Series editions, which is principally designed to convey sense to a reader. Actors who find this too cumbersome are encouraged to take the commas and semicolons supplied throughout these editions lightly. In the preparation of copy for Elizabethan printers and in the setting of that copy in the presses, it was usually scribes and compositors rather than playwrights who made decisions about where such punctuation marks appeared. In the theatre, such choices are still up to actors. We hope that these editions will make them clearer.

We hope these editions illuminate and explain Shakespeare's texts without imposing any specific ideas about how to inhabit, perform, read or enjoy them. Our aim throughout has been to set our actor-readers' imaginations free.

Thanks to:

Margaret Bartley who had faith in the idea and has worked tirelessly to see it realized.

The Bloomsbury Arden team for their support and expertise.

The Arden Third Series volume editors whose expertise has provided us with authoritative, modernized editions.

Ralph Alan Cohen, The American Shakespeare Center, our Series Advisor.

Michael Dobson, Abigail Rokison-Woodall,
Simon Russell Beale

ACKNOWLEDGEMENTS

A most particular thanks to Mark Oughton, who brought both the eye of an actor and the hand of a formatting wizard to the draft. Thanks to Wendy Strehlow, Michael Booker, Will Sharpe, Erin Sebo, Felicity Blake and Elliot Moriarty for their comments, freely offered resources, wisdom and support.

SERIES INTRODUCTION

Actors working with modern editions often run up against editorial decisions which may affect their interpretations. Editorial principles for lineation and punctuation are not always made explicit, and are frequently consigned to the discursive notes at the beginning or end of the text. The principles for the selection of particular textual variants vary between editions, and the possible choices available to the actor are not always immediately apparent.

This edition seeks to open the text to actors, making clear those instances where there is a genuine choice in terms of textual variants, and leaving the lineation of the text as open as possible.

PUNCTUATION

- The punctuation of this edition is that of the Arden 3 text, since this is designed to convey the sense most clearly.
- No extant text of Shakespeare represents the author's own punctuation.
- Even the punctuation of early quarto editions thought to have been printed from an authorial manuscript is likely, for the most part, to have originated with the scribes and compositors who were responsible for the transcription and printing of these copies.
- In some cases the punctuation in the Folio is as heavy, or heavier, than that of many modern edited texts.
- With this in mind it seems arbitrary to pick a particular early modern text from which to take the punctuation – this creates as many problems as it solves.

- Actors are not obliged to follow the punctuation of the text in delivery. They may find that it is sometimes better to phrase according to the metre.

- In cases where the punctuation of an early quarto or Folio seems particularly useful or interesting in providing an indication of a character's mood or thought patterns, we provide a facing-page note.

LINEATION

- The lineation of the edition is, again, based on that of Arden 3.

- However, in cases where the lineation is ambiguous, a facing-page note to this effect is added.

- Where the metrical connection between lines seems unambiguous – so-called shared lines – this edition follow George Steevens and editors since 1793 in indenting the second part of the line in order to make the connection visually explicit.

- In cases where three part-lines succeed one another, each pair appearing to have an equal metrical claim to linkage, this edition does not follow the common editorial practice of representing such lines as one shared and one short line. Instead we make the ambiguous metrical connection apparent by indenting both the second and third portions of the line, thus:

MARCELLUS
    Holla Barnardo!
BARNARDO   Say, what, is Horatio there?
HORATIO   A piece of him

                       (*Ham.* 1.1.17)

- In cases where one of the lines might be regarded as an overlapping or interjecting line outside the metrical structure of the scene, we add a note on the facing page, as in this example from *Hamlet*:

HAMLET
    . . . A cut-purse of the Empire and the rule,
    That from a shelf the precious Diadem stole
    And put it in his pocket.
GERTRUDE   No more.
HAMLET   A King of shreds and patches,
                          (*Ham.* 3.4.97–100)

Hamlet's lines could be considered to be continuous with Gertrude's line overlapping. This form of overlap would have been easily indicated to the Renaissance actor working from a cue part by giving the actor playing Hamlet a continuous speech, and the actor playing Gertrude the cue-line 'in his pocket'.

- Where more than three short lines succeed one another and the metrical connection is ambiguous, all lines are aligned to the left hand margin and a note is added.

- This form of lineation is partly motivated by historical evidence suggesting that early modern actors, because of the nature of the scripts they worked with, would not have been able to see the metrical connections between their lines and those of other speakers, and are therefore unlikely to have distinguished between full-line and short-line cues in their delivery.

METRE

- Whilst the dominant metre of Shakespeare's verse is iambic pentameter (five feet per line), Shakespeare increasingly varies this metre, introducing other feet. A note on the metre with more details of metrical variants is provided in the section 'A Note on Metre'.

Long and short lines

- Although most lines have ten (or eleven) syllables, some lines have more or less than this.

- In some instances it is possible to make a line scan as a line of pentameter by eliding a word, for example 'even' being pronounced as one syllable (sometimes represented in editions as e'en).

- In other cases the metre suggests the expansion of a word, for example the pronunciation of 'intermission' as five syllables (**in**-ter-**miss**-i-**on**).

- Facing-page notes are given to alert the actor to such metrical indications.

- The notes indicate the equivalent number of syllables suggested by the metre; for example:

even (equiv. 1 syl.)

in-ter-**miss**-i-**on** (equiv. 5 syl.)

- Bold type in these notes indicates stressed syllables.

- In some cases what appears to be a long line can be scanned by substituting an anapest for an iambic foot. In such cases a facing-page note is provided. The section 'A Note on Metre' explains the use of the anapest.

- Finally, some lines cannot be easily scanned as pentameters. In such cases we provide a facing-page note indicating that a line is either short or long. There is no expectation that the actor will change his or her delivery.

- In a few cases a line of nine syllables is clearly missing the first stressed syllable. This is called a 'headless foot' and its presence is noted in a facing-page note.

- In some cases the verse form suggests that a word might be pronounced differently from its usual sound in both present-day and early modern everyday speech.

- In the case of words ending in 'ed', the metre sometimes suggests that the ending should be pronounced as an extra syllable. In such cases the 'ed' ending is given a grave accent – èd – viz. examinèd.

- In cases where the metre does not suggest the pronunciation of the word-ending as a separate syllable, the word is printed – 'd' – viz. examin'd.

- The aim throughout is to inform and assist rather than to dictate, and the pronunciation of words is, of course, a matter of individual choice.

PRONUNCIATION

- In cases of unusual words or names, this edition provides a guide to pronunciation in a facing-page note (preceded by 'Pron.').

- Pronunciation of character names is given in the *Dramatis Personae* (and not thereafter in the text).

- In cases where a word is used several times, varying in scansion according to the metre, a note is given in the Introduction (and not for each use in the text).

TEXTUAL VARIANTS

- Some of Shakespeare's plays were printed in two or more different early editions.

- Thirty-six of Shakespeare's plays were published in the First Folio of 1623. Prior to the publication of the Folio, eighteen of these plays had appeared individually in quarto form.

- *Pericles* and *The Two Noble Kinsmen* – not included in the First Folio – were also printed in quarto form.

- Some of the quarto texts differ little from their Folio counterparts. In other cases the differences are substantial.

- In most cases there are some variations in terms of individual words.

- Some of these are merely representative of an error of transcription or printing.

- However, in other cases differences between the early texts present the actor with a genuine choice. In such instances we make clear the textual variants in a facing-page note.

Q – indicates a quarto variant

F – indicates a Folio variant

Q1 – First quarto, Q2 – Second quarto, etc.

F1 – First Folio, F2 – Second Folio, etc.

Qq – all authoritative quartos

- In a few cases the quarto and Folio texts contain obvious errors – the result of misreadings, damaged copy or error. In many cases these were emended by eighteenth-century editors. Where this is the case a facing-page note makes the editorial emendation apparent:

Rowe – Nicholas Rowe, 1709

Pope – Alexander Pope, 1725

Theobald – Lewis Theobald, 1733

Hanmer – Thomas Hanmer, 1744

Warburton – William Warburton, 1747

Johnson – Samuel Johnson, 1765

Capell – Edward Capell, 1768

Steevens – George Steevens, 1773

Malone – Edmond Malone, 1790

- Each individual edition provides a clear summary of the variant texts and notes any major textual differences.

SCENE LOCATIONS

- About two-thirds of scenes in Shakespeare plays written for the Globe are unlocated. No indication is given of their precise locale even in the dialogue, and in no early text does an announcement on the page at the beginning of a scene specify where it is taking place.

- When location is important to a scene, Shakespeare usually has characters (or a chorus) vocalize it – for example, 'Well, this is the forest of Arden' (*As You Like It*, 1.4.12), 'The orchard walls are high and hard to climb' (*Romeo and Juliet*, 2.2.63), 'Unto Southampton do we shift our scene' (*Henry V*, 2.0.42).

- As a result, we have resisted the temptation to provide arbitrary locations for scenes.

- The setting of a scene is clearly a matter for each individual production to define (or to leave as ambiguous).

- In texts where scenes have clearly defined locations, these are discussed in the introduction to that edition.

SCENE DIVISIONS

- The early printed quartos contain no act or scene divisions and there is no indication that a play like *Hamlet* was conceived by Shakespeare as being in five acts.

- Act and scene divisions originate with the First Folio. However, in *Hamlet* these are not consistent, appearing sporadically through the first two acts, and then stopping altogether.

- It was with the Quarto of 1676 that act and scene breaks were first introduced into the play, and these have been followed by most editors ever since.

- However, this Quarto introduced a puzzling act and scene division between 3.4 and 4.1, the action of which seems to occur consecutively within the Queen's closet.

- We follow this act and scene division only for the sake of cross-referencing with the many editions and works of criticism which have reluctantly followed this mistake since.

STAGE DIRECTIONS (SD)

- This edition follows the stage directions given in the Arden 3 text.

- The early printed texts of Shakespeare's plays contain relatively few stage directions.

- Where stage directions do not appear in the early texts but have been added by subsequent editors, they are presented in brackets – i.e. [*Exit PHILOSTRATE*].

- There are a few cases in the Folio or quarto texts where a character is instructed to enter in a stage direction, but does not speak. In such cases we provide a facing-page note. The decision as to whether a character who does not speak is to be included in the scene is a matter for each production to determine.

- There are a number of instances in the Folio text of what have been termed 'anticipated entrances' – where a character is instructed to enter on stage before they are required to speak. These entrances may simply indicate the time taken for an actor to get from the back to the front of the Globe stage. However, in some cases they suggest an interesting possibility that a character is seen by the onstage characters before they speak or overhears the onstage action. In such cases we provide a facing-page note indicating the position of the entrance in the Folio (or occasionally Quarto) text.

YOU AND THOU

- In early modern England the pronouns 'you' and 'thou' each served a distinctive function, much like the French equivalents 'vous' and 'tu'.

- Having earlier been the standard form of address, 'thou' became a 'special' pronoun, used affectionately to indicate closeness between speakers, used derogatively in order to patronize or vituperate, and used when addressing allegorical figures, gods or the dead.

- As well as being the plural, 'you' was the more respectful form of address.

- Individual editions contain a brief note on the most significant uses of personal pronouns in the play.

RHETORIC

- Rhetoric – the art of verbal persuasion, studied and codified since classical times – exerted a powerful influence on Elizabethan writing, and rhetorical devices abound in the work of Shakespeare and his contemporaries.

- Some of the most common rhetorical devices are alliteration, assonance, various patterns of repetition, and especially antithesis, which Shakespeare uses frequently to balance lines and to counterbalance clauses, setting light against dark, love against hate, and so on.

RHYME

- Shakespeare uses rhyme in various ways in his plays, the most common being for songs and for rhyming couplets – sometimes isolated, sometimes formed into speeches.

- In Shakespeare's early plays, one of the most common uses of the rhyming couplet is to end a scene.

- In his later plays these final couplets are less common. Sometimes a scene finishes on a couplet followed by a short line which gives a different momentum to an exeunt.

- Couplets are also used to end speeches, adding a flourish to their conclusion.

- A further use of rhyme comes in the form of aphorisms, where characters seem to be coining or citing pithy generalizations.

- One difficulty for the modern actor is that changes in pronunciation from the early modern period to the present day mean that lines that once rhymed do so no longer.

- In such cases we provide a facing-page note. An actor is free to ignore the rhyme and pronounce the words as they are commonly spoken or to employ a deliberately anti-quated delivery in order to point up the rhyme.

VERSE AND PROSE

- Most of Shakespeare's plays are written in a mixture of verse and prose.

- *Henry VI Parts 1* and *3* (c. 1591), *Richard II* (c. 1595) and *King John* (c. 1596) are written entirely in verse.

- *The Merry Wives of Windsor* has the highest proportion of prose – 90 per cent.
- The characters who most often speak prose are:
  - servants, clowns, sailors and workingmen;
  - upper-class characters coming into contact with working-class characters;
  - foreign characters;
  - drunken characters;
  - characters experiencing madness and psychological imbalance;
  - characters in disguise.
- Prose is commonly used for lesser subject matter than verse and for comic dialogue.
- The majority of letters and proclamations are in prose.
- A move from verse to prose within a scene often marks a significant change in tone. There is an increasing tendency in the process of Shakespeare's career to modulate from one medium to another within a scene.

  Where a scene moves from verse to prose or vice-versa, this is indicated in a facing-page note.
- During Shakespeare's career his use of prose becomes more varied, and prose is more often spoken by characters from the upper classes.
- It is sometimes difficult to distinguish between verse and prose. This may be deliberate. In such cases we provide a facing-page note.
- Each individual edition provides a summary of the key uses of verse and prose in the play.

SOURCES

- Many of Shakespeare's plays are based on pre-existing sources – ancient texts such as Plutarch's *Parallel Lives*, classical poems, historical chronicles, earlier plays and stories.

- Shakespeare regularly made alterations to his source material, either in order to make it more theatrical, to make it more shocking (as in the case of the tragic ending which only Shakespeare gives to the well-known legend of King Lear), or to make it more politically and socially relevant.

- It can be misleading for an actor to explore the source material for a text as a means of discovering more about a character, particularly in the case of historical figures: an attempt to play Shakespeare's Richard III as though the play were a documentary about the historical Richard III, for example, is likely to produce contradictory and undramatic results.

- Nevertheless, it can be interesting to note the changes made, and to know some of what Shakespeare was deliberately leaving out or transforming.

- As a point of interest, each edition provides a list of key sources for the play.

- Where there is a clear and significant source for a particular reference, we provide a facing-page note in the text, marked 'Source'.

Proverbial sayings

- Shakespeare's characters often use proverbs.

- Some characters make conscious use of common sayings – sometimes to the point of cliché.

- Others deliberately manipulate well-known aphorisms.

- Since it seems useful for actors to be aware of when a character is consciously using proverbial language, key proverbial sayings are marked 'Prov.'.

Biblical allusions

- Characters in Shakespeare's plays frequently quote from or refer to the Bible.

- Such references would have been more familiar to early modern actors and audiences.

- Again, it seems useful for actors to be aware of when their character is invoking the Bible.

- Biblical allusions are marked 'Bib.'.

LIST OF ABBREVIATIONS

SI – Series Introduction
Intro. – Introduction
Myth – Key figures of classical mythology
Bib. – biblical
equiv. – equivalent to
Pron. – pronunciation
Prov. – proverbial
Punct. – punctuation
SD – stage direction
SP – speech prefix
syl. – syllable/syllables

Michael Dobson, Abigail Rokison-Woodall,
Simon Russell Beale, *Series Editors*

A NOTE ON METRE

Shakespeare's basic metre is iambic pentameter. Iambic pentameter is made up of five feet (a foot being a unit of verse
made up of stressed and unstressed syllables) comprising an
unstressed syllable followed by a stressed syllable, annotated
thus: u /. A regular line of iambic pentameter is scanned as
follows:

   u /   u / u /   u /   u /

HERMIA
   I would my father look'd but with my eyes.

                    (*A Midsummer Night's Dream*, 1.1.56)

Although iambic pentameter forms the basis of Shakespeare's
metre, his metrical line admits a number of variations, particularly as his career progresses.

The essential difficulty with the introduction of iambic
pentameter to the English language was that English language
has inherent stresses. We pronounce 'inherent' as 'in **her** ent'
not '**in** her **ent**', for example. When iambic pentameter was
first introduced into the English language, many poets could
see little alternative but to use it in a regular fashion. George
Gascoigne, in his 'Certayne Notes of Instruction concerning
the making of verse of rhyme in English' (1575), one of the
first English publications on metre, instructs the poet that
'euen in this playne foote of two syllables [he or she should]
wreste no woorde from his natural and vsuall sounde' (George
Gascoigne, 'Certayne Notes of Instruction concerning the
making of verse or rhyme in English' in *The posies of George
Gascoigne Esquire* (London, 1575, 50)).

He gives the following example:

> I understand your meanying by your eye
> Your meaning I understand by your eye

commenting that,

> in these two verses there seemeth no difference at all, since the one hath the very selfe same woordes that the other hath, and yet the latter verse is neyther true nor pleasant, and the first verse may passe the musters.
>
> (Gascoigne, 50–1)

And yet Shakespeare and his contemporaries could not always compose sentences in alternate stresses (this would have become tedious), and thus they began to introduce variants, three of the most common being:

1. The trochee – a foot composed of a stressed syllable followed by an unstressed syllable (/ u). An example might be the first foot of this line:

/   u   u /   u   / u / u /

Friendship is constant in all other things

(Much Ado, 2.1.160)

2. The Spondee – a foot composed of two stressed syllables (/ /). An example might be the first foot of this line:

/   /   u / u / u   / u   /

Hence! home, you idle creatures, get you home:

(Julius Caesar, 1.1.1)

3. The Anapest – a foot composed of two unstressed syllables followed by a stressed syllable (u u /). An example might be the first foot of this line:

u u / u   /   u   /   u / u   /

Be it so she will not here, before your Grace,

(A Midsummer Night's Dream, 1.1.39)

Many lines in Shakespearean drama that might otherwise be considered irregular can be scanned by substituting one of these metrical feet for an iamb. In many cases the scansion is subjective. Whilst one person may wish to speak the following line:

HORATIO
What, has this thing appear'd again tonight?

(*Ham.* 1.1.19)

scanning 'What, has' as an iamb (with the stress on 'has'), another might wish to scan it as a trochee (with the stress on 'What') and another as a spondee (with the stress on 'What' and 'has').

In the case of trochees and spondees, the substitution of one of these feet for an iamb does not affect the overall syllable count of a line, and thus we do not regularly give an indication of where we feel such feet might be present.

There are a few instances in Shakespeare's work of full lines of trochaic rather than iambic metre. Most frequently these are present in Shakespeare's 'magic' metre – when he is writing dialogue for the fairies in *A Midsummer Night's Dream* or for the witches in *Macbeth*. However, they sometimes occur elsewhere in the plays, and their presence is noted, for example, in *Romeo and Juliet*:

Romeo, humours, madman, passion, lover,

(2.1.7)

However, the anapest incorporates an extra syllable into a line, making it appear irregularly long if one does not acknowledge the possibility of this foot. In cases where a line can be made to scan as five feet by the inclusion of an anapest, we note this in a facing-page note.

A more extreme example, similar to an anapest, is the quartus paeon, a foot which comprises three unstressed syllables followed by a stressed syllable (u u u /). In most cases the presence or otherwise of a quartus paeon is ambiguous, and a line might equally be scanned as a deliberate hexameter (six feet), as in the following example.

This line can be scanned with the third foot (quish-er as by) as a quartus paeon:

```
u    / u    / u  u  u / u  /   u  /
Had he been vanquisher, as by the same co-mart
```
(Hamlet, 1.1.90)

or as a deliberate hexameter:

```
u    / u    / u / u / u  /   u  /
Had he been vanquisher, as by the same co-mart
```
(Hamlet, 1.1.90)

Some critics suggest that hexameters are rare and that it is preferable to attempt regularization where possible (E. A. Abbott, *A Shakeseparean Grammar*, 397). Others freely admit the presence of hexameters (George T. Wright, *Shakespeare's Metrical Art*, Chapter 9).

There are sometimes a number of possible ways of scanning a particular line. In the following example, either the second (-lling shall not lack) or third (Let us go in) foot might be scanned as a quartus paeon, or the line can be regarded as a hexameter (with a feminine ending).

God willing shall not lack. Let us go in together
(Hamlet, 1.5.192)

In other cases, scanning a line as a hexameter seems the only logical choice:

He heareth not, he stirreth not, he moveth not;
(Romeo and Juliet, 2.1.15)

SHORT LINES

Headless lines

A common variation on the regular iambic pentameter line is
that of the 'headless' line. A fairly common metrical device in
Shakespeare's work, the headless line is a line that is missing
the first unstressed syllable:

```
(u) /   u  / u /     /     u u  /
```
   Melted as the snow, seems to me now

              (*A Midsummer Night's Dream*, 4.1.166)

```
         (u) /     u  /
```
HORATIO   Where, my lord?

```
                        u / u     / u / u
```
HAMLET   In my mind's eye, Horatio.

              (*Hamlet*, 1.2.185)

Missing beats at the caesura

A further variation on the short verse line is the line in which
a beat appears to be missing at the caesura. The caesura is the
strong mid-line break in a line of verse, often marked by the
end of a phrase or sentence.

If the missing beat is an unstressed beat, this is termed a
'broken-backed line'; for example:

```
u   /   u /  (u) / u    /   u   /
```
To hide the slain?   O, from this time forth

              (*Hamlet*, 4.4.66)

Other lines may be missing a stressed syllable at the mid-
line caesura:

```
u   / u   /   u (/) u /   u /
```
As he would draw it. Long stay'd he so;

(Hamlet, 2.1.87)

FEMININE ENDINGS/TRIPLE ENDINGS

The regular iambic pentameter line consists of five feet, each made up of an unstressed syllable followed by a stressed syllable. One of the most common variations on this line is the presence of what is commonly termed a feminine (or unstressed) ending. A feminine ending consists of an extra unstressed syllable at the end of the ten syllable line, for example:

```
u  / u  / u /   /  u u   /    u
```
To be, or not to be – that is the question;

(Hamlet, 3.1.54)

Occasionally a line ends with two additional unstressed syllables – termed a triple ending:

```
u  / u    /   u /    u /   u /  u u
```
And tediousness the limbs and outward flourishes.

(Hamlet, 2.2.91)

In this case, 'flourishes' may be seen as equivalent to two syllables.

INTRODUCTION

Shakespeare understood that to love is to risk everything. People react in different ways to risk: they might protect themselves with humour, defensiveness or sarcasm. They might find ostentatious ways to declare themselves, but crumble at the first challenge. They might find depths and strengths unimagined in themselves. They might just find themselves transformed. We demand that people in love show it in certain, prescribed ways, but does that risk judging love by how well someone can perform it? Can we trust a performance? That, too, is a risk.

Every beloved screwball comedy owes a debt to *Much Ado About Nothing*. A romantic comedy built around competitive, eroticized quarrelling will always find a way to connect with its audience. The zest, warmth and exuberance of this text allow the audience to travel alongside the developing relationships, and so to feel how they grow and solidify. This play, in contrast to many of the period, or indeed of our own time, treasures women's voices, and their integrity. It is a story where we see a man giving his support to women when they are humiliated and disbelieved. When there are people who are working so hard, as many are at present, to move the conversation surrounding men's violence against women away from policing women's behaviour and towards getting men to support women's voices, this moment in theatre is startlingly apt. Productions should not be afraid of Shakespeare's pointed jests about the unreliability of young men, as he builds them into an ultimately positive message. If man is inconstant, this is what makes him capable of change. If men and women challenge each other, this shows a belief in each other's strength. 'Thou and I are too wise to woo peaceably' is a fine motto. Sound hearts live under prickly exteriors.

THE VARIANT TEXTS

Much Ado About Nothing was probably written in 1598, placing it towards the end of the reign of Queen Elizabeth I, and just before the famous clown of Shakespeare's company, Will Kempe (for whom the part of Dogberry was written), left the Chamberlain's Men. It was first printed in 1600. There are only two key early printed texts:

- Quarto (Q) – published in 1600, from Shakespeare's foul papers.
- First Folio (F1) – published in 1623, printed from a copy of the quarto.

A quarto was a small, usually cheap, book, so called because the printer made it by folding the large sheet of standard paper into quarters. About half of Shakespeare's plays were printed in quarto, sometimes in multiple editions. In the case of this play, only one edition is extant, which simplifies editorial choices. Later, his 'complete works' were gathered together and printed in folio. A folio was a grander, more expensive kind of book, twice the size of a quarto, with the printers' sheet of paper being folded only once. Shakespeare's First Folio was printed in 1623, seven years after his death. 'Foul papers' is the term given to the author's own manuscript (as distinct from copies written up by a scribe). As Q appears to be set from Shakespeare's foul papers, and F is set from Q, with some light annotation, this text is one of the more stable we have.

THIS TEXT/PUNCTUATION

The text of this edition is based on that found in the Arden 3 series, edited by Claire McEachern, which privileges Q except in cases of clear error. The Arden 3 punctuation, similarly, is most reliant on the Quarto as a guide, but with some needful regularizing, such as converting to full stops instances where the Quarto tends to use a colon.

The following editions are also referred to in the text:

Bevington – ed. David Bevington (Bantam Shakespeare) (New York, 1988)
Capell – ed. Edward Capell, 10 vols. (1767–8)
Knight – ed. Charles Knight, 8 vols. (1839–42)
Oxford – ed. Sheldon P. Zitner (Oxford, 1993)

MAJOR TEXTUAL DIFFERENCES

The only textual difference beyond single-word amendments (some obvious corrections, others newly introduced errors or insignificant variations) between the two versions is the removal of two short passages that appear in the Q but not F. Both of these are likely to have been removed in order to avoid giving offence. While this play was written during the reign of Elizabeth I, the First Folio was published under James I, who had differing ideas about what was acceptable on the stage.

A censorship act passed by Parliament in 1606 threatened to fine actors for the misuse of 'the holy name of God'. This explains comfortably the excision of Dogberry's exchange with Borachio and Conrade at 4.2.19–22:

CONRADE, BORACHIO
Yea, sir, we hope.
DOGBERRY
Write down, that they hope they serve God; and write God first, for God defend but God should go before such villains.

A performance at court for the Scottish King James and his Danish Queen, and probable international guests, may have made it discreet to remove Don Pedro's mocking of Benedick's imitation of foreign fashions, at 3.2.31–4:

or in the shape of two countries at once, as a German from the waist downward, all slops, and a Spaniard from the hip upward, no doublet.

VERSE AND PROSE IN THE PLAY

The text leans more heavily towards prose than almost any other of Shakespeare's plays. Only *The Merry Wives of Windsor* has more. These two plays have in common a setting and central plot that are particularly realistic for a Shakespearean comedy – no magic, invented places or outrageous coincidences. While it adheres to convention that the comic characters (Dogberry, Verges and the members of the watch) speak in prose, it is more unusual for the characters of higher social rank to use prose as much as they do here. For much of the early part of the play Claudio takes on the responsibility of reminding the audience that matters of romance and courtship are usually done in verse. When verse does appear in this play it is for the most part quite regular. The only repeated quirk is a tendency towards occasional twelve-syllable lines, and most of these lend themselves to sounding regular when spoken so as to include an anapest, allowing a compressed, quick rhythm over a portion of the line. 'A**gainst** that **power** that **bred** it; **there** [will she] **hide** her' (3.1.11) will sound like a conventional verse line with a feminine ending.

It is a highly distinctive choice to have upper-class characters speak in prose during scenes of romantic declaration, as Beatrice and Benedick do in 4.1 and 5.2. This denies actors many of the useful indicators of phrasing and emphasis embedded in a blank verse text. However, it does give the performer tremendous freedom to make their own decisions about rhythm and emphasis. It suggests Shakespeare's great confidence in the skills of his actors. Only a playwright who trusted his actors implicitly would hand them such a free rein.

Because prose dominates throughout, this edition includes a facing-page note whenever a passage in verse is introduced.

FEMININE ENDINGS

Feminine endings, where an otherwise even iambic pentameter has a single extra, unstressed beat at the end, can be used to create variety and a sense of natural motion in a speech, but at other times may have a more specific purpose. A high frequency of feminine endings can suggest a speaker who is uncertain, confused, deceptive or emotionally unstable. In this play, feminine endings are scattered throughout, rather than tending to be grouped around a particular speaker, so what becomes more notable is their absence. When characters speak with conviction, like Hero when she rejects the accusations against her, the intermittent feminine endings tend to fall away, making statements sound strikingly firm: 'I talk'd with no man at that hour, my lord' (4.1.86).

OTHER METRES AND RHYME

Don Pedro and Hero's brief exchange in 2.1 is cleverer than it appears at first glance. The metre of their four lines (two long lines of fourteen syllables, broken into eight and then six) replicates the 'fourteeners' of Arthur Golding's translation of Ovid's *Metamorphoses*, which is also the source for their literary allusion regarding Philemon. So their poem references not only the content but the form of a well known work dwelling on love and transformative power. In this edition the lineation has been altered on these lines to show where the metre falls.

The song 'Sigh no more' in 2.3 is a modification of simple ballad measure, with an AB rhyme pattern in consistent, alternating tetrameters and triameters, but with the twist of an extra unstressed foot at the end of each triam.

The rites of mourning for Hero's supposed death (5.3) create the only lengthy variation to the play's combination of blank verse and prose. The epitaph and song are based around catalectic trochaic tetrameters (see 'A Note on Metre'). When Claudio and Don Pedro revert to iambic pentameter to converse, they do so in rhyme.

PRONUNCIATION OF KEY WORDS

Pronunciations of place names and archaic words are given as they arise in the text. Character names, if they appear in a passage of verse, must often be considered in conjunction with the scansion of the line. In order to fit in with the rhythms of blank verse, the pronunciation of personal names tends to be very elastic. The same name will be pronounced sometimes with two syllables (in effect, Beer-trice, Claw-dyo) and sometimes three (Bee-at-rice, Claw-di-oh), depending on the metrical requirements of the line. Beatrice, Margaret and Claudio are particularly subject to this.

AMBIGUOUS METRICAL CONNECTIONS

Occasionally, especially in scenes of confrontation or clamour, there may be several short lines in sequence in the middle of a passage of verse. In this play they occur during the broken wedding in 4.1, and the challenges and revelations of 5.1. When this manifests as three short lines in a row, the lines have been stepped to show more clearly the choices available on how they could be connected metrically when spoken.

ANTONIO
    And this is all.
LEONATO   But brother Anthony –
ANTONIO   Come, 'tis no matter.

                              (5.1.99)

When the ambiguity extends over more than three lines, all lines are aligned to the left-hand margin (as indicated in the Series Introduction).[1]

AMBIGUOUS SPEECH PREFIXES

Scenes that include the Watch have required editors to make some decisions about how to distribute lines among the named and unnamed characters. In 3.3 the original texts use 'Watch' or 'Watch 1' and 'Watch 2' for all lines except those of Dogberry and Verges. Following the Arden 3, this edition assigns some lines to Seacoal, who is named during the scene as the man in charge of the Watch. In 4.2, both Q and F, presumably following Shakespeare's hand in the draft they were working from, interpolate the names of the actors Will Kemp and Richard Cowley for the parts they played, Dogberry and Verges, along with several other irregularities in the speech prefixes. Some assignment of lines is therefore the result of editorial decisions to clarify an ambiguous original.

During the dancing in 2.1, both Q and F assign the first three lines of the man in conversation with Margaret to Benedick, then give Balthasar the final two, thus:

BENEDICK
Well, I would you did like me.
MARGARET
So would not I, for your own sake, for I have many ill qualities.
BENEDICK
Which is one?

---

1 For a more lengthy discussion, see Abigail Rokison, *Shakespearean Verse Speaking: Text and Performance* (Cambridge: Cambridge University Press, 2010).

MARGARET

I say my prayers aloud.

BENEDICK

I love you the better; the hearers may cry amen!

MARGARET

God match me with a good dancer!

BALTHASAR

Amen!

MARGARET

And God keep him out of my sight when the dance is done! Answer, clerk.

BALTHASAR

No more words; the clerk is answered.

Most editors have reassigned the full exchange to Balthasar, to make the scene a consistent series of pairs, concluding with Beatrice and Benedick. Some productions prefer to assign the lines to Borachio, in order to set up the link between them, ready for the impending deception.

In 5.3, Claudio converses with an unnamed Lord who reads aloud the epitaph composed for Hero. Afterwards it is this Lord who says,

Now unto thy bones good night;
Yearly will I do this rite.

These lines might seem more appropriately reassigned to Claudio.

In the final scene (5.4), Leonato speaks for Antonio, and then possibly for Benedick, but in both cases the line makes perfectly acceptable, though different, sense left as the original text specifies. 'This same is she and I do give you her' (5.4.54) has often been passed to Antonio, as he is supposed to be the father of the substitute bride. However, as Leonato has declared her his heir, and she is supposedly replacing his daughter in marriage to Claudio, his speaking the line does not seem inappropriate. 'Peace! I will stop your mouth' (5.4.97) is Leonato's in both Q and F, but has usually been reassigned by editors and directors to Benedick. In staging terms, there is no reason why Leonato cannot be the one to indicate that the couple should kiss, and this option does remove the uncomfortable sense of a man seeking to silence his woman, which would be out of character in the moment. It can also be amended to 'mouths'.

AMBIGUOUS ENTRANCES

The scene of revels in 2.1 lacks some necessary entrances in the stage directions. Margaret and Ursula speak at lines 90 and 101 respectively, but their entrances are not marked. They may enter with the revellers at line 75, or at the beginning of the scene, if an emphasis on Leonato's household as a unified group, distinct from the soldiers, is preferred. Later in the same scene, at line 192, this edition suggests an entrance for Don Pedro, Hero and Leonato. The original stage directions, however, offer '*Enter the Prince, Hero, Leonato, John and Borachio and Conrade*' in Q, but only '*Enter the Prince*' in F. The Folio then suggests '*Enter Claudio and Beatrice, Leonato, Hero*' at line 240. The difference would be whether a production wishes Leonato and Hero to hear Benedick's exchange with the Prince about Claudio's disgruntlement and Beatrice's perceived faults.

YOU AND THOU

You, as well as being a plural, is more formal and more appropriate to someone not well known or of higher rank to the speaker. Thou is used with intimate companions, relatives, younger persons, or sometimes to servants. A shift in usage alters the tone of the conversation. Here, for example, everybody uses 'you' throughout the opening scene, as we see a series of greetings and public exchanges. Then when everyone else has left them alone, the first use of 'thou' in the play comes from Claudio, drawing Benedick into an intimate conversation about his feelings for Hero. When Don Pedro returns he uses 'thou' with both, but Benedick continues with 'you' to both his companions, perhaps underlining his continued separation from their position, as they discuss love and marriage. The same pattern is apparent in 5.1, when Don Pedro and Claudio attempt to include Benedick in their boisterous humour, but he instead makes his challenge to Claudio, and officially distances himself from them.

It is the Prince's prerogative to use the intimate form of address with his subjects, which he does freely, but no one uses 'thou' and 'thee' in response to him. When making his offer of marriage to Beatrice, however, Don Pedro reverts to the more formal 'you'.

Beatrice and Benedick maintain the formal 'you' throughout their early scenes of banter. Benedick uses 'you' for his first declaration of love at 4.1.267, but then progresses to 'thee', while Beatrice continues to use 'you' with him. This imbalance is kept all through their later meeting in 5.2, and even in the final scene.

At 2.2.50, Borachio refers to his superior, Don John, as 'you' in Q, but this was altered to 'thou' in F.

GHOST CHARACTERS

In the stage directions at the start of Act 1 and Act 2 the group entrance includes mention of Leonato's wife (given in the first stage direction as '*Innogen his wife*' and in the second simply as '*his wife*'). There need be no purposeful explanation of why she is listed and yet has no lines; playwrights worked fast in this period, and it would be completely normal for Shakespeare to plan out a scene, note down the characters, then find one unnecessary but forget to remove her from the stage directions. Equally, however, Innogen might be seen as part of a pattern of introducing characters who are related to our major players, but who never appear. Leonato mentions Claudio's uncle in Messina, and 1.2 begins with yet another mention of a relative who does not speak, Antonio's son. The play does much to suggest a wider world built of a network of relationships. This helps emphasize that any decision someone makes (to marry, to break a union, to duel) they make for their family, not just for themselves.

SOURCES

The plot of a woman unjustly slandered, who almost loses her reputation and her marriage before being vindicated, was a popular one in the early modern period, so Hero and Claudio have many antecedents. The most secure sources for the Hero and Claudio plot are probably a story in Ludovico Ariosto's *Orlando Furioso*, and a prose novella by Matteo Bandello which was made available to Shakespeare's contemporaries in a French version by François de Belleforest in his *Histories Tragiques*. Ariosto's tale of a Scottish princess called Genevra and her Italian suitor Ariodante was popular enough to see many spin-off translations and versions, so was highly likely to be known by Shakespeare, though the Bandello/Belleforest story maps more closely onto *Much Ado*, in being set in Messina with a father figure called Lionato. The story of a couple tricked into falling in love in the manner of Beatrice and Benedick may have been Shakespeare's own invention. If there was an earlier version of this scenario in circulation at the time of writing it has not been identified.

RHETORIC

Although there is no known direct source for the Beatrice and Benedick plot, Shakespeare owes much to the earlier writer John Lyly for the nature of their back-and-forth relationship. McEachern's delightfully descriptive phrase 'allusive citation'[2] best describes the debt to Lyly's *Euphues: The Anatomy of Wit* and *Euphues and his England* – Shakespeare does not imitate so much as riff on his precepts, for an audience who likely represented a shared fandom. Understanding euphuistic principles derived from Lyly's work, and earlier rhetoricians forming a chain all the ways back to Cicero, unlocks multiple aspects of this play otherwise easy to miss. Everyone is taking part in an interlinked sequence of rhetorical games. There are purposes besides mere entertainment that layer themselves on these exchanges. Courtship is only the most obvious. In the case of Don Pedro and Leonato's formal yet affectionate first meeting, these excessively courteous greetings serve to establish their mutually respectful relationship, while at the same time ironically foreshadowing the troubles to come. Dogberry does accidentally what Beatrice does deliberately, when he continually responds to people's words as if they meant something else. Margaret and Balthasar's attempts to enter the game show social ambition.

To the modern ear there is no question but that euphuistic dialogue sounds like flirting. There are numerous scenes besides those between Beatrice and Benedick that still read as (potentially sexually charged) flirtatious banter. That is, flirtation not of compliment, but of challenge. It is effective to see the interactions between Beatrice and Benedick as the key link in a network of such exchanges: Beatrice flirts combatively

---

2   Claire McEachern, *Much Ado About Nothing*, Arden 3 edition (London: Bloomsbury, 2015), p. 77.

with Benedick, there is something similar going on between Benedick and Margaret, and between Margaret and Balthasar, the same between Balthasar and Don Pedro, and Don Pedro back to Beatrice again. The mirror image of all this verbal competitiveness is the almost complete silence with which Claudio and Hero conduct their wooing.

WIT

In modern usage we take wit to mean sharp humour, but at the time of writing it more often meant intelligence or wisdom (as opposed to folly), or referred to a person's mental faculties. Given that it is sharp rejoinders that Beatrice and Benedick are known for among their friends, however, we can see already forming the association of the old with the newer meanings. When Beatrice responds to Leonato's description of their 'skirmish of wit' she flips the sense of the word from repartee to abilities of mind. The 'five wits' in question were common sense, imagination, fantasy, estimation and memory.[3] The word wit and its variants is played with constantly throughout, so alertness to multiple meanings will be rewarded.

JOKES

A major question when making textual cuts for production of this play is how much of the 'old' humour to leave in. There are jokes that still work, jokes that work with the judicious alteration of a word or two, jokes that work with a delivery that conveys the meaning, and jokes that will likely only ever perplex. The point of the joke is often embedded in the general

---

3 Stephen Hawes, *The Passetyme of Pleasure* (1509).

knowledge shared by members of Shakespeare's society. For instance, when Benedick speaks of Claudio thrusting his neck into a yoke like an ox, his first audience would have known that the oxen have horns like a cuckold, are whipped, and are joined by the yoke in pairs, making them multiple signifiers of a married man. Or when Beatrice says her Uncle's fool 'subscribed for Cupid', an audience aware of the different varieties of archery competition would see that the significance is that Benedick's challenge is not answered by a man of rank or skill. Benedick wanted to beat Cupid, the world's most famous archer whom he openly despises (in Cupid's role as god of love) at long-distance archery, but instead the only person who would show up to compete with him was a fool with a blunt arrow. On the other hand, all that really matters in performance when Benedick refuses to trust his 'bugle' to an 'invisible baldrick' is that it sounds convincingly rude.

Changes in pronunciation can also affect how much humour is picked up by a listening audience. At the time of this play's first performances, the word 'nothing' was pronounced similarly to 'noting', and here lies the crux of much punning humour sprinkled throughout. The action is driven by every possible form of 'noting', in terms of observing (watching, taking note of, or reflecting on). In addition, it is Hero's 'no thing' that there is much ado about – this was a common euphemism for women's genitals, both as referring to the lack of a 'thing' and the presence of a shape like a zero. The many jokes about musical notation also form part of this matrix of puns.

OATHS

This play is full of commonplace oaths that add more to mood than meaning: 'by my troth', 'marry', 'i'faith', 'go to', 'what the goodyear', and so on. Common oaths can vary in what they imply, depending on the context – 'marry' is short for 'by [the Virgin] Mary', and therefore an affirmation, but while most often used as a substitute for 'indeed', at other times it is more like 'truthfully'.

ALLEGORICAL FIGURES

Whenever an abstract noun is given a capital we are in the presence of an allegorical figure. Harking back to classical deities, it was common to think of virtues, vices and forces of nature as having a human embodiment. The ladies Disdain, Courtesy, Scorn, Beauty, Nature, Tongue and Fame all appear in this play, along with the gentlemen Repentance and Knavery, and even Don Worm the conscience. When the Watch think Deformed is a person, a co-conspirator of Borachio's, it makes a jest at this convention. The watchmen enact literally what their superiors have been using as a rhetorical device – the image of an abstract idea represented in an actual person.

HUMOURS

Much reference is made to people's natural dispositions. A balance of the four humours (choleric, phlegmatic, sanguine and melancholy) created a personality. It is the presence or absence of the sombre melancholy element that preoccupies these characters, especially.

RACE

There are two lines with unfortunate racist implications, typical of the period. Elizabethan England did not trouble itself about the feelings of foreigners or the ethnically marginalized, unless they were ambassadorial dignitaries. The first such line is when Benedick says, 'If I do not love her I am a Jew.' The passage is in prose, so a word can be substituted or the line can be cut at will, without disrupting a metre. The second line is in the final scene when Claudio promises to marry the girl proffered to him 'were she an Ethiope' (5.4.38). Keeping only the first half of the line, 'I'll hold my mind', creates a short line, but makes perfectly adequate sense.

MASQUE

The device of a masquerade ball allows licensed deception, and permitted confusion of rank and decorum. As a form of entertainment, a masque was a curious event in that it blurred the lines between host, guest and performer. Masks, costume and disguise could be worn by hired professional actors and musicians, but also in rehearsed presentations performed by the host or hostess and their friends, or by everybody present. It meant that people could interact with someone without knowing who they were, but equally granted the opportunity to pretend not to know, even if they did. There is no indication that any of the revellers are disguised as any particular figure, except for a suggestion that Don Pedro is wearing a mask that makes him unattractive ('God defend the lute should be like the case').

A production can choose to provide everybody with masks for the revels in 2.1, or give them only to the men. The dialogue makes it explicit that both the visiting soldiers and at least some of the men of Leonato's household are disguised (see Ursula's exchange with Antonio). If the women are also masked, it will emphasize the carnival atmosphere and suggest that everyone is being freed temporarily from their usual social constraints. It is not made clear by the text whether or not Beatrice realizes it is Benedick she is speaking with, and productions have made the scene work either way.

SOCIAL RANK

Occasional references to heraldic devices help underline the consciousness of rank and its markers that permeates this play. A 'difference' on a coat of arms is that mark that signifies the device belongs to the lesser branch of a family, so if Benedick is bearing the difference, his status is subordinate to that of his horse. Rank is something the exalted can choose to set aside, which will reflect well on their personality, such as when the Prince proposes to Beatrice or suggests to Leonato that they enter together. Those further down the ladder do not have the power to decide that rank is inconsequential.

The class status of Margaret and Ursula is difficult to communicate in modern performance, as we are no longer familiar with the many finely shaded degrees of rank active in the Renaissance. They are not exactly servants, as they participate in social events in Leonato's household as guests, but they would expect to be given orders and tasks, and some social interactions would be closed to them. Women of particularly high status would be attended on by women who were also of good birth, but of lesser social standing. Despite her unclear parentage and fortune, Beatrice expects to have a waiting-gentlewoman rather than be one (2.1.30), so she is clearly of superior breeding.

PUBLIC AND PRIVATE SPACES

This play features many exchanges that derive much of their character from whether they take place in public, in private or in an ambiguous, overlapping situation. At the scene of the broken wedding, Claudio and his friends have made a conscious decision to make Hero's humiliation as public as possible. Consequently, Claudio's repentance must likewise be public. Revenge and contrition must happen where they will be seen – Beatrice does not desire to eat Claudio's heart in the parlour, but in the marketplace. Contrasting scenes of the greatest possible intimacy – three women dressing, close friends making a new confession of desire – are constantly intruded upon by the public. Claudio and Don Pedro's conversation is overheard and reported on (or rather misreported) by a man of Antonio's, and also by Borachio. What Margaret believes to be an intimate encounter with Borachio has been turned by him into a public show. The Prince, Claudio and Leonato, and then Hero and Ursula, make much of their conversations being private, knowing that they are actually making them public, to Benedick and Beatrice respectively.

KEY FIGURES OF CLASSICAL MYTHOLOGY

Ate (**Ah**-tay) (2.1.234) – Greek goddess of discord.

Cupid (1.1.38–9, 1.1.174, 1.1.236, 1.1.252, 2.1.354, 3.1.22, 3.1.106 and 3.2.10) – Greek/Roman god of love. Son of Aphrodite/Venus. Depicted as a cherub or young boy with a bow and arrow, sometimes blindfolded.

Diana (4.1.56 and 5.3.12) – Roman goddess of the moon, the hunt and of chastity. Artemis in the Greek.

Europa (5.4.45–8) – Greek/Roman myth. A human girl kidnapped by Jove/Zeus while he was disguised as a bull.

fury (1.1.182) – Greek/Roman myth. There were three furies, goddesses of vengeance, who pursued and tormented their victims into madness.

harpy (2.1.248) – Greek/Roman myth. Vicious monsters, half bird and half woman.

Hector (2.3.184) – Trojan prince, and the bravest warrior of Troy.

Hercules (**Her**-cue-**lees**) (1.2.153, 2.1.29, 2.1.232, 2.1.337, 3.3.132, 4.1.318 and 5.2.280) – Roman myth. Greek hero (Herakles), son of Zeus. Famous for his strength and courage. Carried out twelve seemingly impossible tasks (the Twelve Labours). Depicted wearing a lion's skin and holding a club. Ovid wrote of his relationship with Queen Omphale, in which they exchanged clothes, while he acted as her servant.

Hero (4.1.80) – Greek myth. Virgin priestess of Aphrodite. Drowned herself when her lover, Leander, died trying to swim across the Hellespont to reach her.

Hymen (**Hi**-men) (5.3.32) – Greek god of marriage.

Jove (3.2.278 and 3.4.54) – Roman king of the gods. Also Jupiter, or Zeus in the Greek

Leander (Lee-**an**-der) (5.2.30) – Greek myth. Lover of Hero (above). Drowned.

Philemon (**Fil**-eh-mon) (2.1.85) – A poor man who, with his wife, gave shelter in his thatched cottage to the disguised Jove and Mercury.

Phoebus (**Fee**-bus) (5.3.26) – Phoebus Apollo. Twin brother of Artemis/Diana. Greek/Roman god of the sun, who drives his chariot across the sky.

Troilus (**Troy**-lus or **Troh**-lus) – Prince of Troy, brother to Hector. In medieval legend he had a doomed romance with Cressida.

Vulcan (1.1.174) – Roman god of the forge, metalwork and blacksmiths.

SUGGESTED FURTHER READING

For further detailed information about the play, we refer the reader to the Arden 3 edition, which contains material on the texts, sources, critical history and performance heritage:

McEachern, Claire. *Much Ado About Nothing*. Arden 3 edition. London: Bloomsbury, 2015.

Further suggestions:

Cox, John F., ed. *Much Ado About Nothing (Shakespeare in Production)*. Cambridge: Cambridge University Press, 1997.

Freedman, Penelope. *Power and Passion in Shakespeare's Pronouns: Interrogating 'you' and 'thou'*. Aldershot: Ashgate, 2007.

Kahan, Jeffrey et al. *Much Ado About Nothing (Sourcebooks Shakespeare)*. London: Methuen, 2007.

Kamaralli, Anna. *Shakespeare and the Shrew: Performing the Defiant Female Voice*. London: Palgrave Macmillan, 2012.

Kesson, Andy. *John Lyly and Early Modern Authorship*. Manchester: Manchester University Press, 2014.

Reeves, Saskia. *Actors on Shakespeare: Much Ado About Nothing*. London: Faber & Faber, 2003.

Rokison, Abigail. *Shakespearean Verse Speaking: Text and Theatre Practice*. Cambridge: Cambridge University Press, 2010.

Wright, George T. *Shakespeare's Metrical Art*. London: University of California Press, 1988.

DRAMATIS PERSONAE

DON PEDRO, Prince of Aragon.

DON JOHN, his bastard brother.

SIGNOR BENEDICK, a lord of Padua.

SIGNOR CLAUDIO, a lord of Florence – Pron. **Claw**-di-**oh** (3 syl.) or **Claw**-dyo (2 syl.).

BALTHASAR, attendant on Don Pedro, a musician – Pron. **Bal**-thuh-zar.

BORACHIO, attendant on Don John – Pron. Bor-**ah**-chee-**oh**.

CONRADE, attendant on Don John – Pron. with either long or short A is acceptable.

LEONATO, Governer of Messina – Pron. **Lee**-on-**ah**-to (4 syl.) or Leeon-**ah**-to (3 syl.) as at 5.4.20.

ANTONIO, brother to Leonato – called Anthony by Leonato at 5.1.

HERO, daughter to Leonato.

BEATRICE, niece to Leonato – Pron. **Bee**-a-**trice** (3 syl.) or **Beer**-trice (2 syl.).

MARGARET, waiting gentlewoman to Hero – Pron. **Marg**-ar-**et** (3 syl.) or **Mar**-gret (2 syl.), called Meg by Hero at 3.4.

URSULA, waiting gentlewoman to Hero – Pron. **Ur**-syu-**lah** (3 syl.) or **Ur**-syula (2 syl.), called Ursley by Hero at 3.1.

DOGBERRY, Constable, in charge of the watch.

VERGES, Headborough, his partner in office – Pron. with soft G.

GEORGE SEACOAL, of the watch.

FRIAR FRANCIS, a priest.

Sexton.

Members of the watch, a boy, messengers, lords, attendants, musicians.

MUCH ADO ABOUT NOTHING

ACT 1, SCENE 1

Enter LEONATO, Governor of Messina, HERO his daughter and
BEATRICE his niece, with a Messenger.

LEONATO

    I learn in this letter that Don Pedro of Aragon
    comes this night to Messina.

MESSENGER

    He is very near by this. He was not three
    leagues off when I left him.

LEONATO

    How many gentlemen have you lost in this   5
    action?

MESSENGER

    But few of any sort, and none of name.

LEONATO

    A victory is twice itself when the achiever
    brings home full numbers. I find here that Don Pedro
    hath bestowed much honour on a young Florentine   10
    called Claudio.

MESSENGER

    Much deserved on his part, and equally
    remembered by Don Pedro. He hath borne himself
    beyond the promise of his age, doing in the figure of a
    lamb the feats of a lion; he hath indeed better bettered   15
    expectation than you must expect of me to tell you how.

SD Q/F – *LEONATO Governor of Messina, INNOGEN his wife* (see Intro.)

Aragon – *kingdom in northern Spain*   Q – Pedro F – Peter
Messina (Mess-**een**-ah) – *town in Sicily (then part of the Spanish Empire)*

by this – *by now/according to this letter*; three leagues – *around 9 miles*

action – *military encounter*

sort – *kind/rank*; name – *noble family/reputation*

achiever – *victor*
full numbers – *i.e. no casualties*

equally remembered – *acknowledged as deserved*

better bettered expectation – *gone beyond what was hoped of him*

LEONATO

He hath an uncle here in Messina will be very
much glad of it.

MESSENGER

I have already delivered him letters, and
there appears much joy in him, even so much that joy   20
could not show itself modest enough without a badge
of bitterness.

LEONATO

Did he break out into tears?

MESSENGER

In great measure.

LEONATO

A kind overflow of kindness; there are no faces   25
truer than those that are so washed. How much better
is it to weep at joy than to joy at weeping!

BEATRICE

I pray you, is Signor Mountanto returned
from the wars or no?

MESSENGER

I know none of that name, lady; there was   30
none such in the army of any sort.

LEONATO

What is he that you ask for, niece?

HERO

My cousin means Signor Benedick of Padua.

joy . . . modest – *decorum called for a moderating element in his show of joy*
badge – *public marker*

kind . . . kindness – *pun on 'kind' as generous/kindred; overflow – excess*

pray – *ask of;* Mountanto – *an upward thrust in fencing*

MESSENGER
> O, he's returned, and as pleasant as ever he
> was.   35

BEATRICE
> He set up his bills here in Messina and
> challenged Cupid at the flight; and my uncle's fool,
> reading the challenge, subscribed for Cupid and
> challenged him at the bird-bolt. I pray you, how many
> hath he killed and eaten in these wars? But how many   40
> hath he killed? For indeed I promised to eat all of his
> killing.

LEONATO
> Faith, niece, you tax Signor Benedick too
> much, but he'll be meet with you, I doubt it not.

MESSENGER
> He hath done good service, lady, in these   45
> wars.

BEATRICE
> You had musty victual, and he hath holp to
> eat it. He is a very valiant trencher-man: he hath an
> excellent stomach.

MESSENGER
> And a good soldier too, lady.   50

BEATRICE
> And a good soldier to a lady; but what is he to
> a lord?

pleasant – *agreeable*

bills – *notices of challenge (for an archery competition)*
flight – *long-distance archery contest*; fool – *jester/a sly self-deprecating reference?*
subscribed for Cupid – *signed up to represent Cupid* (see Myth)
bird-bolt – *a short, blunt arrow*
how . . . wars – *(an intention to kill and eat the enemy demonstrates manly fervour)*

Faith – *By my faith (truly)*; tax – *take to task*
meet – *pay you back the same amount*

musty victual – *stale provisions*; holp – *helped*   F – victual Q – vittaile
trencher-man – *hearty eater*
stomach – *courage (but Beatrice jokes that for him it means appetite)*

to a lady – *when compared to a lady*

MESSENGER
    A lord to a lord, a man to a man, stuffed
    with all honourable virtues.

BEATRICE
    It is so indeed, he is no less than a stuffed man;   55
    but for the stuffing – well, we are all mortal.

LEONATO
    You must not, sir, mistake my niece; there is a
    kind of merry war betwixt Signor Benedick and her.
    They never meet but there's a skirmish of wit between
    them.   60

BEATRICE
    Alas, he gets nothing by that. In our last
    conflict, four of his five wits went halting off, and now
    is the whole man governed with one, so that if he have
    wit enough to keep himself warm, let him bear it for a
    difference between himself and his horse, for it is all the   65
    wealth that he hath left to be known a reasonable
    creature. Who is his companion now? He hath every
    month a new sworn brother.

MESSENGER
    Is't possible?

BEATRICE
    Very easily possible. He wears his faith but as   70
    the fashion of his hat: it ever changes with the next
    block.

MESSENGER
    I see, lady, the gentleman is not in your
    books.

stuffed – *fortified*

stuffed – *scarecrow/dummy/puffed-up/fat/empty of true heart and guts*
but . . . stuffing – *as to what he is stuffed with*   Punct. stuffing – well Q/F – stuffing
well

gets – *wins*; that – *i.e. battling her*
five wits – *mental faculties*; halting – *limping*

wit . . . warm – *sense enough to come in from the cold*; bear it – *carry/show*; for – *as*
difference – *mark on a coat of arms indicating the lesser branch of a family*

sworn brother – *chivalric term for a comrade in arms*

faith – *allegiance*

block – *a wooden mould for shaping felt hats according to the fashion*

books – *favour (good books)*

BEATRICE

No; an he were, I would burn my study. But I   75
pray you, who is his companion? Is there no young
squarer now that will make a voyage with him to the
devil?

MESSENGER

He is most in the company of the right noble
Claudio.   80

BEATRICE

O Lord, he will hang upon him like a disease!
He is sooner caught than the pestilence, and the taker
runs presently mad. God help the noble Claudio! If he
have caught the Benedick, it will cost him a thousand
pound ere 'a be cured.   85

MESSENGER

I will hold friends with you, lady.

BEATRICE

Do, good friend.

LEONATO

You will never run mad, niece.

BEATRICE

No, not till a hot January.

MESSENGER

Don Pedro is approached.   90

an – *if*
pray you – *beg of you*
squarer – *one eager for a quarrel (as in, to 'square off')*
will . . . devil – *will swear alliance through the most perilous enterprise*

sooner – *more easily*; pestilence – *plague*; taker – *one taken ill*
presently – *immediately*
cost . . . cured – *Benedicts were priests paid to perform exorcisms*   Q – Benedict
ere – *before*; 'a – *he*   Q –'a F – he F2 – it

I . . . you – *I will be careful to stay on your good side*

run mad – *catch the Benedick/chase after men*   Q – You will never F – You'll ne're

is approached – *has arrived*

Enter DON PEDRO, CLAUDIO, BENEDICK, BALTHASAR and
[DON] JOHN the bastard.

DON PEDRO
  Good Signor Leonato, are you come to meet
  your trouble? The fashion of the world is to avoid cost,
  and you encounter it.

LEONATO
  Never came trouble to my house in the likeness
  of your grace, for, trouble being gone, comfort should   95
  remain; but when you depart from me, sorrow abides,
  and happiness takes his leave.

DON PEDRO
  You embrace your charge too willingly. I
  think this is your daughter.

LEONATO
  Her mother hath many times told me so.   100

BENEDICK
  Were you in doubt, sir, that you asked her?

LEONATO
  Signor Benedick, no, for then were you a child.

DON PEDRO
  You have it full, Benedick; we may guess by
  this what you are, being a man. Truly, the lady fathers
  herself. Be happy, lady, for you are like an honourable   105
  father. [*Don Pedro and Leonato walk apart.*]

fashion – *preference*

charge – *task/cost*

for . . . child – *i.e. Benedick was not yet busy trying to sleep with everyone's wives*

You . . . full – *You have been fully answered*
lady fathers herself – *her looks make it clear who her father is*

BENEDICK

> If Signor Leonato be her father, she would
> not have his head on her shoulders for all Messina, as
> like him as she is.

BEATRICE

> I wonder that you will still be talking, Signor   110
> Benedick; nobody marks you.

BENEDICK

> What, my dear Lady Disdain! Are you yet
> living?

BEATRICE

> Is it possible Disdain should die, while she
> hath such meet food to feed it as Signor Benedick?   115
> Courtesy itself must convert to Disdain if you come in
> her presence.

BENEDICK

> Then is Courtesy a turncoat. But it is certain
> I am loved of all ladies, only you excepted; and I would
> I could find in my heart that I had not a hard heart,   120
> for truly I love none.

BEATRICE

> A dear happiness to women – they would else
> have been troubled with a pernicious suitor. I thank
> God and my cold blood, I am of your humour for that:
> I had rather hear my dog bark at a crow, than a man   125
> swear he loves me.

BENEDICK

> God keep your ladyship still in that mind,

have . . . shoulders – *want to look like an old man* (Prov. 'old head on young shoulders')

marks – *notices/registers what you say*

Lady Disdain – *allegorical embodiment of the characteristic*

meet – *appropriate/fit (pun on meat)*

dear happiness – *stroke of good luck*

of your humour – *share your temperament*

so some gentleman or other shall scape a predestinate
scratched face.

BEATRICE

Scratching could not make it worse, an 'twere   130
such a face as yours were.

BENEDICK

Well, you are a rare parrot-teacher.

BEATRICE

A bird of my tongue is better than a beast of
yours.

BENEDICK

I would my horse had the speed of your   135
tongue, and so good a continuer. But keep your way,
o'God's name; I have done.

BEATRICE

You always end with a jade's trick; I know you
of old.

DON PEDRO

That is the sum of all, Leonato. [*Addresses the*   140
company.] Signor Claudio and Signor Benedick, my
dear friend Leonato hath invited you all. I tell him we
shall stay here at the least a month, and he heartily
prays some occasion may detain us longer. I dare swear
he is no hypocrite, but prays from his heart.   145

LEONATO

If you swear, my lord, you shall not be forsworn.
[*to Don John*] Let me bid you welcome, my lord, being

scape – *escape*; predestinate – *preordained/inevitable*

an 'twere – *if it were*

parrot-teacher – *one who repeats phrases over so a parrot will learn to say them*

better – *(beasts being incapable of speech/if the beast is a snake his tongue is forked/deceiving)*

continuer – *of great stamina/able to go on for a long time*; keep your way – *carry on as you are*

jade – *a wayward horse/hack*

sum of all – *full story (Don Pedro has been updating Leonato during the above exchange)*

prays – *asks*

If . . . forsworn – *(a simple affirming of the truth of Don Pedro's statement)*

reconciled to the prince your brother. I owe you all
duty.

DON JOHN
I thank you. I am not of many words, but I   150
thank you.

LEONATO
[*to Don Pedro*] Please it your grace lead on?

DON PEDRO
Your hand, Leonato; we will go together.

Exeunt all but Benedick and Claudio.

CLAUDIO
Benedick, didst thou note the daughter of
Signor Leonato?   155

BENEDICK
I noted her not, but I looked on her.

CLAUDIO
Is she not a modest young lady?

BENEDICK
Do you question me as an honest man should
do, for my simple true judgement? Or would you have
me speak after my custom, as being a professed tyrant   160
to their sex?

CLAUDIO
No, I pray thee, speak in sober judgement.

reconciled – *i.e. since Don John has been reconciled to the Prince, Leonato must be too*

we . . . together – *an act of courtesy from Don Pedro, who outranks Leonato*

noted her not – *took no particular notice of her*

professed – *well-known/avowed*; tyrant to – *slanderer of*

BENEDICK

Why, i'faith methinks she's too low for a high
praise, too brown for a fair praise and too little for a
great praise. Only this commendation I can afford her: 165
that were she other than she is, she were unhandsome;
and being no other but as she is, I do not like her.

CLAUDIO

Thou thinkest I am in sport. I pray thee tell me
truly how thou lik'st her.

BENEDICK

Would you buy her that you inquire after her? 170

CLAUDIO

Can the world buy such a jewel?

BENEDICK

Yea, and a case to put it into. But speak you
this with a sad brow? Or do you play the flouting jack,
to tell us Cupid is a good hare-finder and Vulcan a rare
carpenter? Come, in what key shall a man take you to 175
go in the song?

CLAUDIO

In mine eye, she is the sweetest lady that ever
I looked on.

BENEDICK

I can see yet without spectacles, and I see no
such matter. There's her cousin, an she were not 180
possessed with a fury, exceeds her as much in beauty as
the first of May doth the last of December. But I hope
you have no intent to turn husband – have you?

i'faith – *in faith (truthfully)*; methinks – *it seems to me*

in sport – *making a game*

Yea – *Yes* (Pron. yay); case – *vagina (making jewel equate with virginity)*
flouting jack – *scornful trickster*
Cupid ... Vulcan – (see Myth)
Cupid ... carpenter – *i.e. asking for affirmation of qualities patently not present*
go – *join in/follow along*

I can see – *(I/eye makes an aural pun)*
her cousin – *i.e. Beatrice*; an – *if*
fury – *tormenting, maddening goddesses in Greek mythology* (see Myth)

CLAUDIO

    I would scarce trust myself, though I had sworn

    the contrary, if Hero would be my wife.   185

BENEDICK

    Is't come to this? In faith, hath not the world

    one man but he will wear his cap with suspicion? Shall

    I never see a bachelor of threescore again? Go to,

    i'faith. An thou wilt needs thrust thy neck into a yoke,

    wear the print of it and sigh away Sundays. Look, Don 190

    Pedro is returned to seek you.

Enter DON PEDRO.

DON PEDRO

    What secret hath held you here that you

    followed not to Leonato's?

BENEDICK

    I would your grace would constrain me to tell.

DON PEDRO

    I charge thee on thy allegiance.   195

BENEDICK

    You hear, Count Claudio? I can be secret as a

    dumb man; I would have you think so. But on my

    allegiance – mark you this, on my allegiance – he is in

    love. With who? Now, that is your grace's part. Mark

    how short his answer is: with Hero, Leonato's short 200

    daughter.

CLAUDIO

    If this were so, so were it uttered.

scarce . . . contrary – *(to keep his oath)*

hath . . . suspicion – *is there no man who will not risk having his cap conceal cuckolds' horns*

threescore – *sixty*; Go to, i'faith – *(a reprimand)*
An . . . needs – *If you insist on*; yoke – *heavy piece of wood worn by oxen/prisoners*
wear . . . it – *be marked by the imprint*; sigh . . . Sundays – *(now filled by dull domestic pursuits)*

constrain – *compel*

allegiance – *sworn duty to obey*

dumb – *mute*

that is . . . part – *i.e. 'With who?' is the line the Prince should speak*

If . . . uttered – *(Claudio avoids confirming or denying)*

BENEDICK

Like the old tale, my lord: 'it is not so, nor
'twas not so'; but indeed, God forbid it should be so!

CLAUDIO

If my passion change not shortly, God forbid it
should be otherwise.

205

DON PEDRO

Amen, if you love her, for the lady is very
well worthy.

CLAUDIO

You speak this to fetch me in, my lord.

DON PEDRO

By my troth, I speak my thought.

210

CLAUDIO

And in faith, my lord, I spoke mine.

BENEDICK

And by my two faiths and troths, my lord, I
spoke mine.

CLAUDIO

That I love her, I feel.

DON PEDRO

That she is worthy, I know.

215

BENEDICK

That I neither feel how she should be loved

Like the old tale – *denying until the moment proof is revealed* (Prov. tale of Mr Fox)

If . . . shortly – *(extends the verbal play on 'short'/lets slip that his feelings may be conditional)*

Amen – *(religious affirmation)*

fetch me in – *bring me to reveal myself to you*

troth – *truth (by my honest word)*

two . . . troths – *(an honest man, of course, should not have two faiths and truths)*

Q – spoke F – speak

nor know how she should be worthy is the opinion that
fire cannot melt out of me; I will die in it at the stake.

DON PEDRO

Thou wast ever an obstinate heretic in the
despite of beauty.   220

CLAUDIO

And never could maintain his part but in the
force of his will.

BENEDICK

That a woman conceived me, I thank her; that
she brought me up, I likewise give her most humble
thanks; but that I will have a recheat winded in my   225
forehead, or hang my bugle in an invisible baldrick, all
women shall pardon me. Because I will not do them the
wrong to mistrust any, I will do myself the right to trust
none. And the fine is – for the which I may go the finer
– I will live a bachelor.   230

DON PEDRO

I shall see thee, ere I die, look pale with love.

BENEDICK

With anger, with sickness, or with hunger, my
lord, not with love. Prove that ever I lose more blood
with love than I will get again with drinking, pick out
mine eyes with a ballad-maker's pen and hang me up at   235
the door of a brothel-house for the sign of blind Cupid.

DON PEDRO

Well, if ever thou dost fall from this faith,
thou wilt prove a notable argument.

fire . . . stake – *(like a heretic martyr)*

despite – *scorn*

never . . . will – *he maintains his position out of obstinacy, rather then belief*

recheat – *hunting call played on a horn*; winded – *blown*
forehead – *(where cuckolds' horns grow)*; bugle – *horn/penis*; baldrick – *shoulder strap*
pardon me – *a polite no thank you to trusting his penis to an unreliable (invisible) receptacle*

fine – *conclusion/penalty*; go the finer – *be better off/better dressed*

ere – *before*; pale with love – *lovers would be pale with pining*

lose more blood – *lovers' sighs drew blood away from the heart*
get . . . drinking – *drinking provokes a flushed and therefore blood-filled complexion*
ballad-maker's – *lovers were notorious composers of ballads*
for – *to serve as*

notable argument – *noteworthy topic of discussion*

BENEDICK

> If I do, hang me in a bottle like a cat and shoot
> at me, and he that hits me, let him be clapped on the   240
> shoulder and called Adam.

DON PEDRO

> Well, as time shall try. 'In time the savage
> bull doth bear the yoke.'

BENEDICK

> The savage bull may, but if ever the sensible
> Benedick bear it, pluck off the bull's horns and set   245
> them in my forehead; and let me be vilely painted, and
> in such great letters as they write 'Here is good horse
> to hire', let them signify under my sign, 'Here you may
> see Benedick, the married man.'

CLAUDIO

> If this should ever happen, thou wouldst be   250
> horn-mad.

DON PEDRO

> Nay, if Cupid have not spent all his quiver in
> Venice, thou wilt quake for this shortly.

BENEDICK

> I look for an earthquake too, then.

DON PEDRO

> Well, you will temporize with the hours.   255
> In the meantime, good Signor Benedick, repair to
> Leonato's, commend me to him and tell him I will
> not fail him at supper, for indeed he hath made great
> preparation.

bottle – *wicker basket*
let him . . . Adam – *let him be congratulated as the best archer (ref. Adam Bell, a famous outlaw)*

try – *test/prove*
In . . . yoke – *(approximates a prov. quote)*   Source: Thomas Kyd, *The Spanish Tragedy*

sensible – *of good sense/capable of feeling*
bull's horns – *(symbol of the cuckold)*
vilely painted – *depicted in crude style, suitable for a business sign*

horn-mad – *mad like a savage bull/enraged cuckold*

spent – *shot/ejaculated*; quiver – *supply of arrows*; Venice – *(famous for its courtesans)*
quake – *answers quiver/be shaken by passion or the fevers accompanying venereal disease*

earthquake – *(highly unlikely, but more likely to be the thing that shakes him than love)*

temporize – *become more tempered/temperate with time*

BENEDICK

I have almost matter enough in me for such   260
an embassage. And so, I commit you –

CLAUDIO

'To the tuition of God. From my house' – if I
had it –

DON PEDRO

'The sixth of July. Your loving friend,
Benedick.'   265

BENEDICK

Nay, mock not, mock not. The body of your
discourse is sometime guarded with fragments, and the
guards are but slightly basted on neither. Ere you flout
old ends any further, examine your conscience. And so
I leave you.   *Exit.*   270

CLAUDIO

My liege, your highness now may do me good.

DON PEDRO

My love is thine to teach; teach it but how,
And thou shalt see how apt it is to learn
Any hard lesson that may do thee good.

CLAUDIO

Hath Leonato any son, my lord?   275

DON PEDRO

No child but Hero; she's his only heir.
Dost thou affect her, Claudio?

matter – *sense*

embassage – *diplomatic mission*; commit – *entrust*

tuition – *safe keeping*

'To . . . Benedick' – *playing on the epistolary style of exchange by finishing a letter*

body . . . fragments – *the substance of your talk is decorated/trimmed merely by scraps*

slightly basted on – *provisionally stitched (basting holds a piece in place until properly sewn)*

flout old ends – *recite traditional truths mockingly (i.e. ignore proverbial wisdom)*

This is the first point at which the play switches from PROSE to VERSE.

love . . . how – *the love I bear you is at your service, to be instructed as to how to help you*

apt – *eager/predisposed*

Hath . . . son – *(any son would inherit Leonato's estate, rather than his daughter)*

affect – *love*

CLAUDIO   O my lord,
   When you went onward on this ended action
   I look'd upon her with a soldier's eye,
   That lik'd, but had a rougher task in hand   280
   Than to drive liking to the name of love.
   But now I am return'd, and that war-thoughts
   Have left their places vacant, in their rooms
   Come thronging soft and delicate desires,
   All prompting me how fair young Hero is,   285
   Saying I lik'd her ere I went to wars.

DON PEDRO
   Thou wilt be like a lover presently
   And tire the hearer with a book of words.
   If thou dost love fair Hero, cherish it,
   And I will break with her and with her father,   290
   And thou shalt have her. Was't not to this end
   That thou began'st to twist so fine a story?

CLAUDIO
   How sweetly you do minister to love,
   That know love's grief by his complexion!
   But lest my liking might too sudden seem,   295
   I would have salv'd it with a longer treatise.

DON PEDRO
   What need the bridge much broader than the flood?
   The fairest grant is the necessity;
   Look what will serve is fit. 'Tis once, thou lovest,
   And I will fit thee with the remedy.   300
   I know we shall have revelling tonight;
   I will assume thy part in some disguise
   And tell fair Hero I am Claudio;
   And in her bosom I'll unclasp my heart

Metre – either **Clau**-dio is 2 syl. or the 'o's of 'Claudio' and 'O my lord' may overlap
went . . . action – *set out on this now completed mission*

that – *now that*

I lik'd . . . wars – *(the conclusion of this line suggests a 'but', or a trailing off and shrug)*

like a lover – *lovers were infamously loquacious*

break – *broach the question/negotiate*
end – *goal*
twist so fine a story – *construct such a well-crafted speech*

minister – *tend*   Q – you do F – do you
complexion – *appearance*   com-**plex**-i-**on** (equiv. 4 syl.)

salv'd – *soothed by applying balm*; treatise – *a scholarly writing*

flood – *body of water to cross*
fairest . . . fit – *what is required is most appropriate*
'Tis once – *It's settled (once and for all)*

revelling – *rowdy celebrations*

in her bosom – *to her confidence*

And take her hearing prisoner with the force   305
And strong encounter of my amorous tale.
Then after, to her father will I break,
And the conclusion is: she shall be thine.
In practice let us put it presently.

Exeunt.

ACT 1, SCENE 2

Enter LEONATO and [ANTONIO,] an old man,
brother to Leonato[, meeting].

LEONATO
How now, brother, where is my cousin your
son? Hath he provided this music?

ANTONIO
He is very busy about it. But brother, I can tell
you strange news that you yet dreamt not of.

LEONATO
Are they good?   5

ANTONIO
As the event stamps them, but they have a good
cover: they show well outward. The prince and Count
Claudio, walking in a thick-pleached alley in mine
orchard, were thus much overheard by a man of mine:
the prince discovered to Claudio that he loved my niece   10
your daughter, and meant to acknowledge it this night
in a dance; and if he found her accordant, he meant to
take the present time by the top and instantly break
with you of it.

prisoner . . . encounter – *(extended metaphor of a military campaign)*

pris-oner (equiv. 2 syl.)
am-orous (equiv. 2 syl.)

presently – *immediately*

cousin – *used for all close relations beyond immediate family*

strange – *out of the ordinary*

they – *(news is usually plural in Elizabethan usage)*

event . . . cover – *as the outcome shall determine, but they appear good*
stamps . . . cover – *(his series of metaphors is drawn from book binding)*
thick-pleached – *with closely-woven branches*

Q – mine F – my

discovered – *disclosed*

accordant – *agreeable*
by the top – *by the topknot/forelock (i.e. to seize the moment)*

LEONATO
  Hath the fellow any wit that told you this?   15

ANTONIO
  A good sharp fellow; I will send for him, and
  question him yourself.

LEONATO
  No, no; we will hold it as a dream till it appear
  itself. But I will acquaint my daughter withal, that
  she may be the better prepared for an answer, if   20
  peradventure this be true. Go you and tell her of it.

                    [Exit Antonio.]

          [Enter Attendants, and cross the stage.]

  Cousins, you know what you have to do. O, I cry you
  mercy, friend: go you with me and I will use your skill.
  Good cousin, have a care this busy time!

                      Exeunt.

ACT 1, SCENE 3

             Enter DON JOHN the bastard and
                CONRADE his companion.

CONRADE
  What the goodyear, my lord! Why are you thus
  out of measure sad?

DON JOHN
  There is no measure in the occasion that
  breeds, therefore the sadness is without limit.

wit – *sense*

hold ... itself – *treat it as an illusion until it materializes*
aquaint ... answer – *(Hero will be instructed so as to be ready to say yes)*

peradventure – *by chance*

I cry you mercy – *I beg your pardon*

What the goodyear – *Hope for a good year (inoffensive exclamation)*
out of measure – *without proportion*

measure ... breeds – *no limit to the matter causing the sadness*

CONRADE

> You should hear reason.   5

DON JOHN

> And when I have heard it, what blessing
> brings it?

CONRADE

> If not a present remedy, at least a patient
> sufferance.

DON JOHN

> I wonder that thou – being as thou sayst   10
> thou art, born under Saturn – goest about to apply a
> moral medicine to a mortifying mischief. I cannot hide
> what I am. I must be sad when I have cause, and smile
> at no man's jests; eat when I have stomach, and wait
> for no man's leisure; sleep when I am drowsy, and   15
> tend on no man's business; laugh when I am merry,
> and claw no man in his humour.

CONRADE

> Yea, but you must not make the full show of
> this till you may do it without controlment. You have
> of late stood out against your brother, and he hath ta'en 20
> you newly into his grace, where it is impossible you
> should take true root but by the fair weather that
> you make yourself. It is needful that you frame the
> season for your own harvest.

DON JOHN

> I had rather be a canker in a hedge than a rose   25
> in his grace, and it better fits my blood to be disdained
> of all than to fashion a carriage to rob love from any. In

Q – at least F – yet

sufferance – *endurance*

born under Saturn – *i.e. morose and gloomy (saturnine)*
moral . . . mischief – *suggest a philosophical cure for an incurable bodily distemper*

wait . . . leisure – *wait to eat when it suits others as well*

claw . . . humour – *soothe/stroke no man who is in a bad mood (ill humour)*

Yea – *Yes* (Pron. yay)
controlment – *restraint*
stood out against – *rebelled*; ta'en – *taken* (Pron. tane)

frame . . . harvest – *create circumstances that cultivate the result you want*

canker – *wild or dog rose/not cultivated (also a blemished blossom)*

fashion a carriage – *imitate a demeanour*; rob love – *win favour on false pretences*

39

this, though I cannot be said to be a flattering honest
man, it must not be denied but I am a plain-dealing
villain. I am trusted with a muzzle and enfranchised   30
with a clog. Therefore I have decreed not to sing in
my cage. If I had my mouth I would bite; if I had my
liberty I would do my liking. In the meantime, let me
be that I am, and seek not to alter me.

CONRADE

Can you make no use of your discontent?   35

DON JOHN

I make all use of it, for I use it only. Who
comes here?

Enter BORACHIO.

What news, Borachio?

BORACHIO

I came yonder from a great supper. The
prince your brother is royally entertained by Leonato,   40
and I can give you intelligence of an intended marriage.

DON JOHN

Will it serve for any model to build mischief
on? What is he for a fool that betroths himself to
unquietness?

BORACHIO

Marry, it is your brother's right hand.   45

DON JOHN

Who, the most exquisite Claudio?

flattering – *with an implied sense of 'servile'*

muzzle . . . clog – *trusted only under strict limits and restrictions*

If . . . mouth – *If I had the freedom to use my mouth (was unmuzzled)*

no use of – *no profit out of*

Q – I make   F – I will make

yonder – *from over there*

intelligence – *information*

What . . . fool – *What manner of fool is he*
unquietness – *(implying that marriage inevitably brings turmoil)*

Marry – *common mild oath (originally 'by the Virgin Mary')*

exquisite – *perfect/fine*

BORACHIO
Even he.

DON JOHN
A proper squire! And who, and who? Which
way looks he?

BORACHIO
Marry, on Hero, the daughter and heir of   50
Leonato.

DON JOHN
A very forward March chick! How came you
to this?

BORACHIO
Being entertained for a perfumer, as I was
smoking a musty room comes me the prince and   55
Claudio, hand in hand in sad conference. I whipped me
behind the arras, and there heard it agreed upon that
the prince should woo Hero for himself, and having
obtained her, give her to Count Claudio.

DON JOHN
Come, come, let us thither; this may prove   60
food to my displeasure. That young start-up hath all
the glory of my overthrow. If I can cross him any way,
I bless myself every way. You are both sure, and will
assist me?

CONRADE
To the death, my lord.   65

proper – *exemplary*; squire – *knight-in-training/stock figure of an ideal lover*

F – on Q – one

forward March chick – *an early hatchling (i.e. young and getting ahead of itself)*

entertained for a perfumer – *employed to perfume a stuffy room by burning aromatics*

hand in hand – *(a direction to consider for the earlier scene)*; sad – *serious*
arras – *tapestry wall covering*

thither – *there*
start-up – *upstart*; glory . . . overthrow – *(Claudio won advancement by vanquishing John)*
cross – *impede/joke made with subsequent line, to bless himself by crossing himself*
bless – *benefit*; sure – *loyal, firm*

DON JOHN

Let us to the great supper; their cheer is the
greater that I am subdued. Would the cook were o'my
mind. Shall we go prove what's to be done?

BORACHIO

We'll wait upon your lordship.

Exeunt.

ACT 2, SCENE 1

Enter LEONATO, his brother [ANTONIO],
HERO his daughter and BEATRICE his niece.

LEONATO

Was not Count John here at supper?

ANTONIO

I saw him not.

BEATRICE

How tartly that gentleman looks! I never can
see him but I am heart-burned an hour after.

HERO

He is of a very melancholy disposition.   5

BEATRICE

He were an excellent man that were made just
in the midway between him and Benedick: the one is
too like an image and says nothing, and the other too
like my lady's eldest son, evermore tattling.

subdued – *apparently defeated*   Q – o' F – of

Would . . . mind – *I wish the cook's disposition was poisonous, like mine; prove – test*

SD Q/F – *Enter Leonato, his brother, his wife, Hero his daughter and Beatrice his niece*

and a kinsman

tartly – *sour/sharp*

melancholy disposition – *relative balance of the four elements made a personality* (see Intro.)

eldest son – *(the kind of child who would be indulged rather than hushed)*

LEONATO

Then half Signor Benedick's tongue in Count   10
John's mouth, and half Count John's melancholy in
Signor Benedick's face –

BEATRICE

With a good leg and a good foot, uncle, and
money enough in his purse, such a man would win any
woman in the world – if 'a could get her good will.   15

LEONATO

By my troth, niece, thou wilt never get thee a
husband, if thou be so shrewd of thy tongue.

ANTONIO

In faith, she's too curst.

BEATRICE

Too curst is more than curst. I shall lessen
God's sending that way; for it is said 'God sends a curst   20
cow short horns' – but to a cow too curst he sends none.

LEONATO

So, by being too curst, God will send you no
horns.

BEATRICE

Just, if he send me no husband. For the which
blessing I am at him upon my knees every morning and   25
evening. Lord, I could not endure a husband with a
beard on his face! I had rather lie in the woollen.

LEONATO

You may light on a husband that hath no beard.

a good leg – *with shapeliness/grace in dance*

'a – *he*; emphasis is likely on 'if'   Q – 'a F – he

troth – *truth (by my honest word)*
shrewd – *sharp/critical*

curst – *perverse/shrewish*

lessen God's sending – *by being 'too curst' she will be sent even less than the curst*
curst – *angry/fierce*
'God . . . horns' – *Prov.: the aggressive are not granted means to harm*

Just – *Just so/That's right*; no husband – *(the cuckold's horns could be attached to either sex)*
I am . . . knees – *I kneel in gratitude*

lie in the woollen – *lie in blankets without sheets*

Q – on F – upon

BEATRICE

What should I do with him? Dress him in my
apparel and make him my waiting-gentlewoman? He   30
that hath a beard is more than a youth, and he that hath
no beard is less than a man; and he that is more than
a youth is not for me, and he that is less than a man, I
am not for him. Therefore I will even take sixpence in
earnest of the bearward and lead his apes into hell.   35

LEONATO

Well then, go you into hell?

BEATRICE

No, but to the gate, and there will the devil
meet me like an old cuckold with horns on his head,
and say, 'Get you to heaven, Beatrice, get you to heaven.
Here's no place for you maids!' So deliver I up my apes   40
and away to Saint Peter fore the heavens. He shows me
where the bachelors sit, and there live we as merry as
the day is long.

ANTONIO

[*to Hero*] Well, niece, I trust you will be ruled
by your father.   45

BEATRICE

Yes, faith, it is my cousin's duty to make
curtsy, and say, 'Father, as it please you.' But yet for
all that, cousin, let him be a handsome fellow, or else
make another curtsy, and say, 'Father, as it please me.'

LEONATO

Well, niece, I hope to see you one day fitted   50
with a husband.

Dress . . . gentlewoman? – *ref. Omphale's treatment of Hercules* (see Myth)   Source:
Ovid, *Fasti*

take . . . hell – *Prov.: the fate of spinsters in the afterlife was said to be to lead apes in hell*
in earnest – *as downpayment*; bearward – *bear keeper who might also have apes in his charge*
Knight – bearward F3 – bearherd

cuckold – *deceived husband (traditionally depicted as horned)*

maids – *virgins/unmarried girls*
Saint Peter – *keeper of the gates of heaven*; fore – *in front of/'before heaven' is an affirmation*
bachelors – *(a gender-neutral term at this time)*

faith – *truly*; make curtsy – *a deferential, feminine bow*

BEATRICE

Not till God make men of some other metal
than earth. Would it not grieve a woman to be overmastered with a piece of valiant dust? To make an
account of her life to a clod of wayward marl? No,   55
uncle, I'll none. Adam's sons are my brethren, and
truly, I hold it a sin to match in my kindred.

LEONATO

Daughter, remember what I told you. If the
prince do solicit you in that kind, you know your
answer.   60

BEATRICE

The fault will be in the music, cousin, if you be
not wooed in good time. If the prince be too important,
tell him there is measure in everything, and so dance out
the answer. For hear me, Hero; wooing, wedding and
repenting is as a Scotch jig, a measure and a cinque-   65
pace. The first suit is hot and hasty, like a Scotch jig,
and full as fantastical; the wedding mannerly-modest as
a measure, full of state and ancientry; and then comes
Repentance, and with his bad legs falls into the cinque-
pace faster and faster, till he sink into his grave.   70

LEONATO

Cousin, you apprehend passing shrewdly.

BEATRICE

I have a good eye, uncle; I can see a church by
daylight.

LEONATO

[*to Antonio*] The revellers are entering, brother.
Make good room. [*Antonio steps aside, and masks.*]   75

metal – *material/pun on mettle* (substance of character)

overmastered – *(legally men were the masters of their wives)*

dust – *(as God made Adam,* Bib. Genesis 2.7)

wayward – *straying/off the path*; marl – *soil*

Adam's sons – *i.e. all men*

sin ... kindred – *(there were strictly prescribed rules about marriage between related people)*

in that kind – *in the way of a marriage proposal*

in good time – *soon/with the correct rhythm*; important – *pun on exalted/importunate*

measure – *temperance/a sequence of dance steps*

measure – *formal dance, based on set figures*

suit – *pun on romantic suit/musical suite*

full as fantastical – *just as elaborate/wild*

ancientry – *the reverence that comes with age*

his bad legs – *(Repentance is envisioned as an old man)*

cinque-pace (**sin**-ka **pace**) – *dance with 5 steps then a leap (here, into a grave)/pun on sink apace*

apprehend passing shrewdly – *are acute in your understanding*

see ... daylight – *identify what is obvious*

Make good room – *(a useful physical cue)*

Enter DON PEDRO, CLAUDIO, BENEDICK,
BALTHASAR, [masked, with a Drum, MARGARET
and URSULA,] and DON JOHN, [BORACHIO and others.
Music and dancing begin].

DON PEDRO

[*to Hero*] Lady, will you walk a bout with
your friend?

HERO

So you walk softly, and look sweetly, and say nothing,
I am yours for the walk; and especially when I walk away.

DON PEDRO

With me in your company?   80

HERO

I may say so, when I please.

DON PEDRO

And when please you to say so?

HERO

When I like your favour – for God defend the lute
should be like the case!

DON PEDRO

My visor is Philemon's roof: 85
Within the house is Jove.

HERO

Why then, your visor should be thatched.

SD Q/F – Margaret, Ursula have no entrance marked. Here or at the scene start are both viable.

The following exchanges lend themselves to being incorporated into a choreographed dance.

a bout – *a turn around the dance floor/a round of fencing*

So – *If*

may – *might (she may or may not decide to allow him to accompany her)*

favour – *face*; defend – *forbid*; lute – *medieval stringed instrument*
God . . . case – *(implication that he wears an ugly or fearsome mask)*

visor – *mask*
Philemon's . . . Jove – (see Myth)

Source: Ovid, *Metamorphoses*
ll.85–8–Metre – Pedro and Hero speak a little poem of alternating 8 and 6 syl. lines (see Intro.)

thatched – *like a cottage roof*

DON PEDRO
      Speak low if you speak love. [*They move*
      aside; Balthasar and Margaret come forward.]

BALTHASAR
      Well, I would you did like me.

MARGARET
      So would not I, for your own sake, for I have   90
      many ill qualities.

BALTHASAR
      Which is one?

MARGARET
      I say my prayers aloud.

BALTHASAR
      I love you the better; the hearers may cry
      amen!   95

MARGARET
      God match me with a good dancer!

BALTHASAR
      Amen!

MARGARET
      And God keep him out of my sight when the
      dance is done! Answer, clerk.

BALTHASAR
      No more words; the clerk is answered. [*They*   100
      move aside; Ursula and Antonio come forward.]

SP – Balthasar (see Intro.) Q/F – Benedick

SP – Balthasar Q/F – Benedick

prayers aloud – *(Puritans did this, so Margaret jests that she is one of these)*

SP – Balthasar Q/F – Benedick

God . . . dancer – *(a demonstration of what she prays aloud for)*

Answer – *(with 'amen')*; clerk – *the respondent in a liturgy*

is answered – *has been told where he stands*

URSULA

I know you well enough; you are Signor
Antonio.

ANTONIO

At a word, I am not.

URSULA

I know you by the waggling of your head.

ANTONIO

To tell you true, I counterfeit him.   105

URSULA

You could never do him so ill-well, unless you
were the very man. Here's his dry hand up and down.
You are he, you are he!

ANTONIO

At a word, I am not.

URSULA

Come, come, do you think I do not know you by   110
your excellent wit? Can virtue hide itself? Go to, mum;
you are he; graces will appear, and there's an end. [*They
move aside; Benedick and Beatrice come forward.*]

BEATRICE

Will you not tell me who told you so?

BENEDICK

No, you shall pardon me.

BEATRICE

Nor will you not tell me who you are?   115

counterfeit – *imitate*

ill-well – *imitate his faults so accurately*
dry hand – *(indicates her taking his hand)*; up and down – *all over*

At – *In*

Go to, mum – *Silence*
graces . . . end – *good qualities will make themselves apparent, and that's that*

BENEDICK
    Not now.

BEATRICE
    That I was disdainful, and that I had my good
    wit out of *The Hundred Merry Tales*! Well, this was
    Signor Benedick that said so.

BENEDICK
    What's he?   120

BEATRICE
    I am sure you know him well enough.

BENEDICK
    Not I, believe me.

BEATRICE
    Did he never make you laugh?

BENEDICK
    I pray you, what is he?

BEATRICE
    Why he is the prince's jester, a very dull fool;   125
    only his gift is in devising impossible slanders. None but
    libertines delight in him, and the commendation is not
    in his wit but in his villainy, for he both pleases men and
    angers them, and then they laugh at him and beat him.
    I am sure he is in the fleet; I would he had boarded me. 130

BENEDICK
    When I know the gentleman, I'll tell him what
    you say.

The Hundred Merry Tales – a popular book of uncouth humorous stories

jester – *(employed not as a knightly companion, but for amusement)*

libertines – *those without morals*; commendation – *value*
villainy – *malice*   Q – pleases F – pleaseth
beat him – *(court fools were often subjected to beatings)*
in the fleet – *among the crowd*; would – *wish*; boarded me – *attempted an attack (the image is of the women as ships with the men as sailors/pirates)*

BEATRICE

Do, do. He'll but break a comparison or two on
me, which, peradventure not marked, or not laughed
at, strikes him into melancholy, and then there's a   135
partridge wing saved, for the fool will eat no supper
that night. We must follow the leaders.

BENEDICK

In every good thing.

BEATRICE

Nay, if they lead to any ill I will leave them at
the next turning.   140

Dance. Exeunt [all but Don John, Borachio and Claudio].

DON JOHN

Sure my brother is amorous on Hero and hath
withdrawn her father to break with him about it. The
ladies follow her, and but one visor remains.

BORACHIO

[*aside to Don John*] And that is Claudio; I
know him by his bearing.   145

DON JOHN

Are not you Signor Benedick?

CLAUDIO

You know me well. I am he.

DON JOHN

Signor, you are very near my brother in his
love. He is enamoured on Hero. I pray you, dissuade

break a comparison – *(as a jousting knight would break a lance)*
peradventure not marked – *if by chance it is not noticed by his audience*

partridge wing – *the scrawniest but most delicate part of the bird*
follow the leaders – *join the dance*

Nay … ill – *(emphasis on 'ill' to counterpoise 'good')*
turning – *a dance figure/crossroads*

amorous on – *in love with/courting*

but one visor remains – *Claudio (still masked) is the only person left on stage*

bearing – *the way he carries himself*

enamoured on – *in love with*; pray – *beg of*

him from her; she is no equal for his birth. You may do 150
the part of an honest man in it.

CLAUDIO
How know you he loves her?

DON JOHN
I heard him swear his affection.

BORACHIO
So did I too, and he swore he would marry her
tonight. 155

DON JOHN
Come, let us to the banquet.

Exeunt all but Claudio.

CLAUDIO
Thus answer I in name of Benedick,
But hear these ill news with the ears of Claudio.
'Tis certain so; the prince woos for himself.
Friendship is constant in all other things, 160
Save in the office and affairs of love.
Therefore all hearts in love use their own tongues:
Let every eye negotiate for itself,
And trust no agent; for Beauty is a witch
Against whose charms faith melteth into blood. 165
This is an accident of hourly proof
Which I mistrusted not. Farewell, therefore, Hero!

Enter BENEDICK.

BENEDICK
Count Claudio.

Again, Claudio is the one to return the text (briefly) to VERSE.

ev-ery (equiv. 2 syl.); ne-**go**-tiate (equiv. 3 syl.)

-gent; for **Beau** (anapest – see 'A Note on Metre')

blood – *passion*

accident . . . proof – *occurrence proved constantly*

mistrusted – *doubted*　　　　Metre – 12 syl. line, Hero's name throws his rhythm

The scene returns to PROSE.

CLAUDIO

Yea, the same.

BENEDICK

Come, will you go with me?   170

CLAUDIO

Whither?

BENEDICK

Even to the next willow, about your own
business, county. What fashion will you wear the
garland of? About your neck, like an usurer's chain? Or
under your arm, like a lieutenant's scarf? You must   175
wear it one way, for the prince hath got your Hero.

CLAUDIO

I wish him joy of her.

BENEDICK

Why, that's spoken like an honest drover; so
they sell bullocks. But did you think the prince would
have served you thus?   180

CLAUDIO

I pray you leave me.

BENEDICK

Ho, now you strike like the blindman! 'Twas
the boy that stole your meat, and you'll beat the post.

CLAUDIO

If it will not be, I'll leave you.   *Exit.*

Yea – *Yes* (Pron. yay)

Whither – *Where*

willow – *(symbolic of pining lovers)*
county – *interchangeable with Count*   Q – county F – Count
garland – *wreath*; usurer's chain – *symbol of a moneylender*
scarf – *sash*   lieutenant's – Pron. – lef-**ten**-ant's in British usage
got – *obtained (with an ambiguous sense wilfully misinterpreted by Claudio)*

honest . . . bullocks – *cattle trader feigning disinterest in the object of purchase*

beat the post – *i.e. strike at the nearest thing*

BENEDICK

Alas, poor hurt fowl, now will he creep into   185
sedges. But that my Lady Beatrice should know me,
and not know me! The prince's fool – hah! It may be I
go under that title because I am merry. Yea, but so I am
apt to do myself wrong. I am not so reputed; it is the
base, though bitter, disposition of Beatrice that puts the 190
world into her person and so gives me out. Well, I'll be
revenged as I may.

Enter DON PEDRO, HERO [and] LEONATO.

DON PEDRO

Now, signor, where's the count? Did you see
him?

BENEDICK

Troth, my lord, I have played the part of Lady   195
Fame. I found him here as melancholy as a lodge in
a warren. I told him, and I think I told him true, that
your grace had got the good will of this young lady, and
I offered him my company to a willow tree, either to
make him a garland, as being forsaken, or to bind him   200
up a rod, as being worthy to be whipped.

DON PEDRO

To be whipped? What's his fault?

BENEDICK

The flat transgression of a schoolboy, who,
being overjoyed with finding a bird's nest, shows it his
companion, and he steals it.   205

sedges – *reeds suitable for concealing a wounded duck*

go . . . title – *am known as such*; Yea – *Yes* (Pron. yay)

puts . . . person – *imagines everyone thinks as she does*
gives me out – *describes me to others*

SD Q – *Enter the Prince, Hero, Leonato, John and Borachio and Conrade* F – *Enter the Prince*

Troth – *In truth*; Lady Fame – *who spreads news*
lodge in a warren – *isolated hut in a game reserve*

Q – think I told F – think, told

rod – *implement for beating schoolboys (usually birch)*

flat – *plain*

DON PEDRO

Wilt thou make a trust a transgression? The
transgression is in the stealer.

BENEDICK

Yet it had not been amiss the rod had been
made, and the garland too; for the garland he might
have worn himself, and the rod he might have bestowed 210
on you, who, as I take it, have stolen his bird's nest.

DON PEDRO

I will but teach them to sing, and restore
them to the owner.

BENEDICK

If their singing answer your saying, by my
faith you say honestly.   215

DON PEDRO

The Lady Beatrice hath a quarrel to you.
The gentleman that danced with her told her she is
much wronged by you.

BENEDICK

O, she misused me past the endurance of a
block! An oak but with one green leaf on it would have 220
answered her; my very visor began to assume life and
scold with her! She told me, not thinking I had been
myself, that I was the prince's jester, that I was duller
than a great thaw, huddling jest upon jest with such
impossible conveyance upon me that I stood like a man 225
at a mark, with a whole army shooting at me. She
speaks poniards, and every word stabs. If her breath
were as terrible as her terminations there were no living

had not been amiss – *was not inappropriate*

have bestowed on – *used to beat*

singing . . . saying – *if what they sing confirms what you say*

to – *with*

visor – *mask*
scold – *argue*
duller . . . thaw – *more tedious than the time of year when travel is impossible*
huddling – *layering*
impossible conveyance – *overwhelming dexterity*
man at a mark – *man who shows where the target is for long-distance archery*
poniards – *daggers*
terminations – *pronouncements*

near her, she would infect to the North Star. I would
not marry her though she were endowed with all that   230
Adam had left him before he transgressed. She would
have made Hercules have turned spit, yea, and have
cleft his club to make the fire too. Come, talk not of her,
you shall find her the infernal Ate in good apparel. I
would to God some scholar would conjure her, for   235
certainly while she is here a man may live as quiet in
hell as in a sanctuary, and people sin upon purpose
because they would go thither – so indeed all disquiet,
horror and perturbation follows her.

Enter CLAUDIO *and* BEATRICE.

DON PEDRO
Look, here she comes.   240

BENEDICK
Will your grace command me any service to
the world's end? I will go on the slightest errand now to
the Antipodes that you can devise to send me on. I will
fetch you a toothpicker now from the furthest inch of
Asia; bring you the length of Prester John's foot; fetch   245
you a hair off the Great Cham's beard; do you any
embassage to the Pygmies, rather than hold three words'
conference with this harpy. You have no employment
for me?

DON PEDRO
None, but to desire your good company.   250

BENEDICK
O God, sir, here's a dish I love not; I cannot
endure my Lady Tongue!   *Exit.*

all . . . transgressed – *i.e. Eden* (Bib.)

Hercules . . . spit – *a domestic cooking task (ref. to Omphale, who made Hercules her servant)* (see Myth); cleft – *split*   Source: Ovid, *Fasti*
Ate (**Ah**-tay) – (see Myth); in good apparel – *disguised by fashionable dress*
scholar – *magician (known for raising demons)*; conjure – *magically banish*

would – *wish to*; thither – *there*

SD Q – *Enter Claudio and Beatrice* F – *Enter Claudio and Beatrice, Leonato, Hero*

I will go . . . Pygmies – *(his suggestions all involve fantastical long journeys)*
Antipodes – *opposite end of the earth*   Antipodes – Pron. – An-**tip**-od-ees
toothpicker – *a popular travel souvenir*
Prester John's foot – *a king of medieval legend*
Great Cham – *Mongol Emperor*
Pygmies – *an African people who appeared often in travellers' tales*
harpy – *tormenting bird/woman monster* (see Myth)

Q – my Lady F – this Lady F3 – this Lady's

DON PEDRO

Come, lady, come; you have lost the heart of
Signor Benedick.

BEATRICE

Indeed, my lord, he lent it me awhile, and I   255
gave him use for it, a double heart for his single one.
Marry, once before he won it of me with false dice;
therefore your grace may well say I have lost it.

DON PEDRO

You have put him down, lady, you have put
him down.   260

BEATRICE

So I would not he should do me, my lord, lest I
should prove the mother of fools. I have brought Count
Claudio, whom you sent me to seek.

DON PEDRO

Why, how now, Count? Wherefore are you
sad?   265

CLAUDIO

Not sad, my lord.

DON PEDRO

How then? Sick?

CLAUDIO

Neither, my lord.

BEATRICE

The count is neither sad, nor sick, nor merry,

he . . . awhile – *(hints at a previous liaison)*

use – *interest (pun on purpose)*   Q – his F – a

Marry – *Indeed*; it – *could equally refer to his heart or hers*; false dice – *weighted, used to cheat*

lest . . . fools – *(making 'put down' literal, i.e. putting her down on her back to have sex)*

Wherefore – *Why*

nor well – but civil count, civil as an orange, and   270
something of that jealous complexion.

DON PEDRO

I'faith, lady, I think your blazon to be true;
though I'll be sworn if he be so his conceit is false.
Here, Claudio, I have wooed in thy name, and fair Hero
is won. I have broke with her father, and his good will   275
obtained. Name the day of marriage, and God give
thee joy!

LEONATO

Count, take of me my daughter, and with her
my fortunes. His grace hath made the match, and all
grace say amen to it.   280

BEATRICE

Speak, Count, 'tis your cue.

CLAUDIO

Silence is the perfectest herald of joy; I were
but little happy if I could say how much. Lady, as you
are mine, I am yours. I give away myself for you, and
dote upon the exchange.   285

BEATRICE

Speak, cousin, or, if you cannot, stop his
mouth with a kiss and let not him speak neither.

DON PEDRO

In faith, lady, you have a merry heart.

BEATRICE

Yea, my lord, I thank it, poor fool, it keeps on

civil – Pron. – closer to Seville at this time

jealous complexion – *a bilious yellow*

blazon – *motto accompanying a heraldic device/convention of describing a lover by their parts*
conceit – *understanding*

broke – *broached the matter*

all grace – *all good thoughts*

dote upon – *adore*

Yea – *Yes* (Pron. yay)

the windy side of care. My cousin tells him in his ear   290
that he is in her heart.

CLAUDIO
And so she doth, cousin.

BEATRICE
Good Lord, for alliance! Thus goes everyone
to the world but I, and I am sunburnt. I may sit in a
corner and cry 'Hey-ho for a husband'.   295

DON PEDRO
Lady Beatrice, I will get you one.

BEATRICE
I would rather have one of your father's
getting. Hath your grace ne'er a brother like you? Your
father got excellent husbands, if a maid could come by
them.   300

DON PEDRO
Will you have me, lady?

BEATRICE
No, my lord, unless I might have another for
working days. Your grace is too costly to wear every
day. But I beseech your grace pardon me, I was born to
speak all mirth and no matter.   305

DON PEDRO
Your silence most offends me, and to be
merry best becomes you, for out o'question, you were
born in a merry hour.

windy side – *upwind/out of the way of*   A very explicit SD for Hero

sunburnt – *(which was thought to make a woman less attractive)*
'Hey-ho for a husband' – *Prov. (a ballad)*

getting – *begetting;* ne'er – *never/not*
got – *sired*

beseech – *beg*
matter – *substance*

becomes – *suits;* out o'question – *without doubt*

BEATRICE

No, sure, my lord, my mother cried; but then
there was a star danced, and under that was I born. [*to* 310
Hero and Claudio] Cousins, God give you joy.

LEONATO

Niece, will you look to those things I told you
of?

BEATRICE

I cry you mercy, uncle. [*to Don Pedro*] By your
grace's pardon.   *Exit.* 315

DON PEDRO

By my troth, a pleasant-spirited lady.

LEONATO

There's little of the melancholy element in
her, my lord. She is never sad but when she sleeps, and
not ever sad then; for I have heard my daughter say she
hath often dreamt of unhappiness and waked herself 320
with laughing.

DON PEDRO

She cannot endure to hear tell of a husband.

LEONATO

O, by no means. She mocks all her wooers out
of suit.

DON PEDRO

She were an excellent wife for Benedick.   325

my mother cried – *in labour*

Niece . . . of – *(Beatrice's uncle is possibly getting her discreetly out of the way)*

cry you mercy – *ask your forgiveness*

troth – *truth*

ever – *always*

suit – *proposal/courtship*

LEONATO

    O Lord, my lord, if they were but a week
    married, they would talk themselves mad.

DON PEDRO

    County Claudio, when mean you to go to
    church?

CLAUDIO

    Tomorrow, my lord. Time goes on crutches till   330
    Love have all his rites.

LEONATO

    Not till Monday, my dear son, which is hence
    a just sennight – and a time too brief, too, to have all
    things answer my mind.

DON PEDRO

    Come, you shake the head at so long a   335
    breathing, but I warrant thee, Claudio, the time shall
    not go dully by us. I will, in the interim, undertake one
    of Hercules' labours, which is to bring Signor Benedick
    and the Lady Beatrice into a mountain of affection
    th'one with th'other. I would fain have it a match, and   340
    I doubt not but to fashion it, if you three will but
    minister such assistance as I shall give you direction.

LEONATO

    My lord, I am for you, though it cost me ten
    nights' watchings.

CLAUDIO

    And I, my lord.   345

sennight – *week (seven nights)*
answer my mind – *satisfactory*

breathing – *breathing space/pause*; warrant – *guarantee*

Hercules' labours – *(his twelve labours were superhuman feats,* see Myth*)*

fain – *wish to*
fashion – *shape*

DON PEDRO

And you too, gentle Hero?

HERO

I will do any modest office, my lord, to help my
cousin to a good husband.

DON PEDRO

And Benedick is not the unhopefullest
husband that I know. Thus far can I praise him: he is   350
of a noble strain, of approved valour and confirmed
honesty. I will teach you how to humour your cousin
that she shall fall in love with Benedick; [*to Claudio and
Leonato*] and I, with your two helps, will so practise
on Benedick that, in despite of his quick wit and his   355
queasy stomach, he shall fall in love with Beatrice. If
we can do this, Cupid is no longer an archer; his glory
shall be ours, for we are the only love-gods. Go in with
me and I will tell you my drift.

Exeunt.

ACT 2, SCENE 2

Enter [DON] JOHN and BORACHIO.

DON JOHN

It is so; the Count Claudio shall marry the
daughter of Leonato.

BORACHIO

Yea, my lord, but I can cross it.

unhopefullest – *least promising*

noble strain – *good breeding*
humour – *encourage her to a disposition*

practise on – *perform an action on*

queasy stomach – *fearfulness*

Yea – *Yes* (Pron. yay); cross – *impede*

DON JOHN
    Any bar, any cross, any impediment will be
    medicinable to me. I am sick in displeasure to him, and   5
    whatsoever comes athwart his affection ranges evenly
    with mine. How canst thou cross this marriage?

BORACHIO
    Not honestly, my lord, but so covertly that no
    dishonesty shall appear in me.

DON JOHN
    Show me briefly how.   10

BORACHIO
    I think I told your lordship, a year since, how
    much I am in the favour of Margaret, the waiting-
    gentlewoman to Hero.

DON JOHN
    I remember.

BORACHIO
    I can, at any unseasonable instant of the night,   15
    appoint her to look out at her lady's chamber window.

DON JOHN
    What life is in that to be the death of this
    marriage?

BORACHIO
    The poison of that lies in you to temper. Go
    you to the prince your brother; spare not to tell him that 20
    he hath wronged his honour in marrying the renowned

Any bar, any cross – *(both features of a heraldic coat of arms)*
medicinable – *curative*
comes athwart – *goes against*; affection – *preference*; ranges evenly – *suits*

unseasonable – *unsociable*

temper – *mix*

Claudio – whose estimation do you mightily hold up
– to a contaminated stale, such a one as Hero.

DON JOHN
What proof shall I make of that?

BORACHIO
Proof enough to misuse the prince, to vex   25
Claudio, to undo Hero and kill Leonato. Look you for
any other issue?

DON JOHN
Only to despite them I will endeavour
anything.

BORACHIO
Go, then. Find me a meet hour to draw Don   30
Pedro and the Count Claudio alone. Tell them that you
know that Hero loves me. Intend a kind of zeal both to
the prince and Claudio – as in love of your brother's
honour, who hath made this match, and his friend's
reputation, who is thus like to be cozened with the   35
semblance of a maid – that you have discovered thus.
They will scarcely believe this without trial; offer them
instances, which shall bear no less likelihood than to
see me at her chamber window, hear me call Margaret
'Hero', hear Margaret term me 'Claudio'. And bring   40
them to see this the very night before the intended
wedding (for in the meantime I will so fashion the
matter that Hero shall be absent), and there shall
appear such seeming truth of Hero's disloyalty that
jealousy shall be called assurance, and all the   45
preparation overthrown.

contaminated – *used*; stale – *whore (often one used as a decoy)*

vex – *upset*

despite – *cause them distress*

meet – *fitting*

Intend . . . zeal – *Pretend to an enthusiasm for their good*

cozened – *deceived/seduced*
semblance of a maid – *appearance of a virgin*
trial – *testing of evidence*
instances – *proofs*; shall . . . likelihood – *shall be no less convincing*

hear . . . 'Claudio' – *could be an error, or imply a sexual game of roleplay*

fashion the matter – *arrange things*

$\qquad$ Q – truth F – truths

assurance – *proof*
preparation – *i.e. for the wedding*; overthrown – *abandoned*

DON JOHN
Grow this to what adverse issue it can, I will
put it in practice. Be cunning in the working this and
thy fee is a thousand ducats.

BORACHIO
Be you constant in the accusation and my   50
cunning shall not shame me.

DON JOHN
I will presently go learn their day of marriage.

Exeunt.

ACT 2, SCENE 3

Enter BENEDICK alone.

BENEDICK
Boy!

[Enter Boy.]

BOY
Signor.

BENEDICK
In my chamber window lies a book. Bring it
hither to me in the orchard.

BOY
I am here already, sir.   5

Grow ... can – *Pursue your plan to the worst it can produce*

Be ... accusation – *Stick with the story*   Q – you   F – thou

presently – *now*

hither – *here*

here already – *expresses intention to be swift*

BENEDICK

I know that, but I would have thee hence and
here again.

Exit [Boy].

I do much wonder that one man, seeing how much
another man is a fool when he dedicates his behaviours
to love, will, after he hath laughed at such shallow   10
follies in others, become the argument of his own
scorn by falling in love. And such a man is Claudio. I
have known when there was no music with him but the
drum and the fife, and now had he rather hear the tabor
and the pipe. I have known when he would have walked 15
ten mile afoot to see a good armour, and now will he lie
ten nights awake carving the fashion of a new doublet.
He was wont to speak plain and to the purpose, like
an honest man and a soldier, and now is he turned
ortography; his words are a very fantastical banquet,   20
just so many strange dishes. May I be so converted and
see with these eyes? I cannot tell; I think not. I will not
be sworn but love may transform me to an oyster, but
I'll take my oath on it, till he have made an oyster of me
he shall never make me such a fool. One woman is fair,   25
yet I am well. Another is wise, yet I am well. Another
virtuous, yet I am well. But till all graces be in one
woman, one woman shall not come in my grace. Rich
she shall be, that's certain; wise, or I'll none; virtuous,
or I'll never cheapen her; fair, or I'll never look on her;   30
mild, or come not near me; noble, or not I for an angel.
Of good discourse, an excellent musician, and her hair
shall be of what colour it please God. Hah! The prince
and Monsieur Love. I will hide me in the arbour.
[*Withdraws.*]

hence – *away*

SD no return is marked for the Boy

argument – *point*

tabor – *small drum used to accompany dances* (Pron. **tay**-bor)

armour – *suit of armour*
carving – *imagining the cut of;* doublet – *short, padded jacket (clothing of the court)*
wont – *inclined* (Pron. wohnt)
turned – *i.e. turned to*   Punct. Q/F – (like and honest man and a soldier)
ortography – *the analysis of words*

oyster – *(low on the hierarchy of animals)*

cheapen – *bid for*
noble . . . angel – *pun on two coins (a noble was a third, an angel half a sovereign)*
hair . . . God – *i.e. not artificially dyed*

Monsieur Love – *Claudio (French was already associated with affectation at this time)*

Enter DON PEDRO, LEONATO, CLAUDIO
[and BALTHASAR*], with Music.*

DON PEDRO
Come, shall we hear this music?   35

CLAUDIO
Yea, my good lord. How still the evening is,
As hush'd on purpose to grace harmony!

DON PEDRO
[*aside to Claudio and Leonato*]
See you where Benedick hath hid himself?

CLAUDIO
[*aside*]
O, very well, my lord. The music ended,
We'll fit the kid-fox with a pennyworth.   40

DON PEDRO
Come, Balthasar, we'll hear that song again.

BALTHASAR
O good my lord, tax not so bad a voice
To slander music any more than once.

DON PEDRO
It is the witness still of excellency
To put a strange face on his own perfection.   45
I pray thee sing, and let me woo no more.

BALTHASAR
Because you talk of wooing I will sing,
Since many a wooer doth commence his suit

A brief return to VERSE.

Yea – *Yes* (Pron. yay)
As . . . harmony – *As if intentionally quiet to facilitate listening to music*

fit . . . pennyworth – *match the cub with what he's earned*

SD Q – *Enter Balthaser with musicke*

tax – *task*

It is . . . perfection – *It is common for the talented performer to protest until persuaded*

woo – *persuade*

-ny a **woo**- (anapest – see 'A Note on Metre')

To her he thinks not worthy, yet he woos,
Yet will he swear he loves.

DON PEDRO   Nay, pray thee, come,   50
Or if thou wilt hold longer argument,
Do it in notes.

BALTHASAR   Note this before my notes:
There's not a note of mine that's worth the noting.

DON PEDRO
Why, these are very crotchets that he speaks.
Note notes forsooth, and nothing!   [*Balthasar plays.*] 55

BENEDICK
Now, divine air! Now is his soul ravished!
Is it not strange that sheep's guts should hale souls out
of men's bodies? Well, a horn for my money, when all's
done.

BALTHASAR (*Sings.*)
Sigh no more, ladies, sigh no more,   60
Men were deceivers ever;
One foot in sea, and one on shore,
To one thing constant never.
Then sigh not so, but let them go,
And be you blithe and bonny,   65
Converting all your sounds of woe
Into 'Hey, nonny, nonny'.
Sing no more ditties, sing no more,
Of dumps so dull and heavy;
The fraud of men was ever so,   70
Since summer first was leavy.

notes – *musical notes* (initiating another round of jokes about noting)

crotchets – *disagreeable things/pun on the musical note*

Metre – line is short by 3 syl.

ravished – *carried off*   The scene returns to PROSE
sheep's guts – *(used to make the strings of instruments)*; hale – *drag*
horn – *(a masculine instrument of hunting or war, rather than love)*

(*Sings.*) – *(no original music is extant)*   Metre – song is in alternating 8/7 syl. lines
(see Intro.)

blithe and bonny – *light spirited and fair*

nonny nonny – *careless frivolities*

dumps – *lows*; dull – *sad*; heavy – *weary*

leavy – *leafy (the new, light leaves of spring)*

Then sigh not so, but let them go,
And be you blithe and bonny,
Converting all your sounds of woe
Into 'Hey, nonny, nonny'.   75

DON PEDRO
By my troth, a good song.

BALTHASAR
And an ill singer, my lord.

DON PEDRO
Ha? No, no, faith; thou sing'st well enough
for a shift.

BENEDICK [*aside*]
An he had been a dog that should have   80
howled thus, they would have hanged him. And I pray
God his bad voice bode no mischief. I had as lief have
heard the night-raven, come what plague could have
come after it.

DON PEDRO
Yea, marry, – dost thou hear, Balthasar? I   85
pray thee get us some excellent music, for tomorrow
night we would have it at the Lady Hero's chamber
window.

BALTHASAR
The best I can, my lord.

DON PEDRO
Do so. Farewell.   *Exit Balthasar.* 90
Come hither, Leonato. What was it you told me of

troth – *truth*

for a shift – *to make do*

An – *if*

bode – *portend*; lief – *willingly*
night-raven – *(harbinger of doom)*

Yea, marry – *(SD indication that he continues conversing while we hear Benedick)*
get – *prepare*

hither – *here*

today? That your niece Beatrice was in love with Signor
Benedick?

CLAUDIO
[*aside*] O ay, stalk on, stalk on, the fowl sits.
[*Raises his voice.*] I did never think that lady would have   95
loved any man.

LEONATO
No, nor I neither. But most wonderful that she
should so dote on Signor Benedick, whom she hath in
all outward behaviours seemed ever to abhor.

BENEDICK
Is't possible? Sits the wind in that corner?   100

LEONATO
By my troth, my lord, I cannot tell what to
think of it. But that she loves him with an enraged
affection, it is past the infinite of thought.

DON PEDRO
Maybe she doth but counterfeit.

CLAUDIO
Faith, like enough.   105

LEONATO
O God! Counterfeit? There was never
counterfeit of passion came so near the life of passion
as she discovers it.

DON PEDRO
Why, what effects of passion shows she?

stalk . . . sits – *the prey is in position, proceed with the hunt*

wonderful – *astonishing*
dote on – *adore*

Sits . . . corner? – *Is that the way the wind blows?*

troth – *truth*
enraged – *passionate*
past . . . thought – *unimaginable*

discovers – *reveals*

CLAUDIO

[*aside*] Bait the hook well, this fish will bite!   110

LEONATO

What effects, my lord? She will sit you – you
heard my daughter tell you how.

CLAUDIO

She did indeed.

DON PEDRO

How, how, I pray you? You amaze me! I
would have thought her spirit had been invincible   115
against all assaults of affection.

LEONATO

I would have sworn it had, my lord; especially
against Benedick.

BENEDICK

I should think this a gull, but that the
white-bearded fellow speaks it. Knavery cannot, sure,   120
hide himself in such reverence.

CLAUDIO

[*aside*] He hath ta'en th'infection; hold it up!

DON PEDRO

Hath she made her affection known to
Benedick?

LEONATO

No, and swears she never will. That's her   125
torment.

She will sit you – *(Leonato begins, but suffers a failure of imagination)*

gull – *trick*
Knavery – *Deviousness*
reverence – *i.e. Leonato's distinguished looks*

He hath . . . infection – *He has taken the bait*

CLAUDIO

'Tis true indeed, so your daughter says. 'Shall
I,' says she, 'that have so oft encountered him with
scorn, write to him that I love him?'

LEONATO

This says she now, when she is beginning to   130
write to him; for she'll be up twenty times a night, and
there will she sit in her smock till she have writ a sheet
of paper. My daughter tells us all.

CLAUDIO

Now you talk of a sheet of paper, I remember a
pretty jest your daughter told us of.   135

LEONATO

O, when she had writ it, and was reading it
over, she found 'Benedick' and 'Beatrice' between the
sheet?

CLAUDIO

That.

LEONATO

O, she tore the letter into a thousand halfpence,   140
railed at herself that she should be so immodest to
write to one that she knew would flout her. 'I measure
him,' says she, 'by my own spirit; for I should flout him,
if he writ to me – yea, though I loved him I should.'

CLAUDIO

Then down upon her knees she falls, weeps,   145
sobs, beats her heart, tears her hair, prays, curses, 'O
sweet Benedick! God give me patience!'

smock – *undergarment worn as petticoat and nightdress*

pretty jest – *amusing joke*

halfpence – *a very small coin*

flout – *scorn*

yea – *yes* (Pron. yay)   Oxford – loved Q/F – love

LEONATO

    She doth indeed; my daughter says so. And the
    ecstasy hath so much overborne her that my daughter
    is sometime afeard she will do a desperate outrage to   150
    herself. It is very true.

DON PEDRO

    It were good that Benedick knew of it by
    some other, if she will not discover it.

CLAUDIO

    To what end? He would make but a sport of it
    and torment the poor lady worse.   155

DON PEDRO

    An he should, it were an alms to hang him.
    She's an excellent sweet lady, and, out of all suspicion,
    she is virtuous.

CLAUDIO

    And she is exceeding wise.

DON PEDRO

    In everything but in loving Benedick.   160

LEONATO

    O my lord, wisdom and blood combating in so
    tender a body, we have ten proofs to one that blood hath
    the victory. I am sorry for her, as I have just cause, being
    her uncle and her guardian.

DON PEDRO

    I would she had bestowed this dotage on me.   165
    I would have doffed all other respects and made her

desperate outrage – *injury*

some other – *someone besides Beatrice herself*

sport – *game*

An – *If*; should – *did*; were – *would be*; alms – *charity*
out of all suspicion – *without question*
virtuous – *chaste*

wisdom . . . victory – *passion always defeats good sense in the young*

dotage – *fondness*
doffed . . . respects – *put off other considerations (such as rank)*

half myself. I pray you tell Benedick of it and hear what
'a will say.

LEONATO
Were it good, think you?

CLAUDIO
Hero thinks surely she will die, for she says she 170
will die if he love her not, and she will die ere she
make her love known, and she will die if he woo her,
rather than she will bate one breath of her accustomed
crossness.

DON PEDRO
She doth well. If she should make tender of 175
her love 'tis very possible he'll scorn it, for the man, as
you know all, hath a contemptible spirit.

CLAUDIO
He is a very proper man.

DON PEDRO
He hath indeed a good outward happiness.

CLAUDIO
Before God, and in my mind very wise. 180

DON PEDRO
He doth indeed show some sparks that are
like wit.

CLAUDIO
And I take him to be valiant.

'a – *he*

Were . . . you? – *Is this a good idea?*

bate – *circumscribe*

doth well – *does the right thing*; make tender – *put forward an offer*

contemptible – *contemptuous (with implication of regrettable)*

proper – *well formed*

hath . . . happiness – *is passably handsome*

Before God – *an affirmation*   Q – Before F – 'fore

show . . . wit – *shows moments that resemble intelligence*

DON PEDRO

As Hector, I assure you. And in the
managing of quarrels you may say he is wise, for either   185
he avoids them with great discretion, or undertakes
them with a most Christian-like fear.

LEONATO

If he do fear God, 'a must necessarily keep
peace; if he break the peace, he ought to enter into a
quarrel with fear and trembling.   190

DON PEDRO

And so will he do, for the man doth fear God,
howsoever it seems not in him by some large jests he
will make. Well, I am sorry for your niece. Shall we go
seek Benedick and tell him of her love?

CLAUDIO

Never tell him, my lord. Let her wear it out   195
with good counsel.

LEONATO

Nay, that's impossible; she may wear her heart
out first.

DON PEDRO

Well, we will hear further of it by your
daughter. Let it cool the while. I love Benedick well,   200
and I could wish he would modestly examine himself to
see how much he is unworthy so good a lady.

LEONATO

My lord, will you walk? Dinner is ready.

Hector – *the bravest Trojan hero* (see Myth)
wise – *sensible*

Christian-like – *(remembering his mortality)*

'a – *he*
if . . . trembling – *(the joke is to praise Benedick for piety by implying he is a coward)*

large jests – *irreverent humour*

wear . . . counsel – *get over it through being advised to do so*

Let . . . while – *In the meantime, give her love time to cool off*

Q – unworthy so F – unworthy to have so

walk – *walk inside*

CLAUDIO

    [*to Don Pedro and Leonato*] If he do not dote on
    her upon this, I will never trust my expectation.   205

DON PEDRO

    [*to Leonato and Claudio*] Let there be the
    same net spread for her, and that must your daughter
    and her gentlewomen carry. The sport will be when
    they hold one an opinion of another's dotage, and no
    such matter. That's the scene that I would see, which   210
    will be merely a dumb-show. Let us send her to call
    him in to dinner.

             [Exeunt all but Benedick.]

BENEDICK

    [*Emerges.*] This can be no trick. The
    conference was sadly borne; they have the truth of this
    from Hero. They seem to pity the lady. It seems her   215
    affections have their full bent. Love me? Why, it must
    be requited. I hear how I am censured: they say I will
    bear myself proudly if I perceive the love come from
    her. They say too that she will rather die than give any
    sign of affection. I did never think to marry. I must not   220
    seem proud; happy are they that hear their detractions
    and can put them to mending. They say the lady is fair
    – 'tis a truth, I can bear them witness. And virtuous –
    'tis so, I cannot reprove it. And wise, but for loving
    me. By my troth, it is no addition to her wit – nor no   225
    great argument of her folly, for I will be horribly in
    love with her. I may chance have some odd quirks and
    remnants of wit broken on me because I have railed so
    long against marriage. But doth not the appetite alter?
    A man loves the meat in his youth that he cannot   230

expectation – *ability to read a situation*

Q – gentlewomen F – gentlewoman

The sport . . . matter – *The fun will be when each believes the other in love, groundlessly*

dumb-show – *mime without words (he assumes they will be confounded into silence)*

sadly borne – *they comported themselves seriously*

full bent – *are at full draw (ref. archery)*

proudly – *as superior*

By my troth – *Truthfully*; no addition . . . wit – *(he admits that loving him might appear foolish);* nor . . . folly – *(he will ensure that her choice is not foolish, by reciprocating)*

endure in his age. Shall quips and sentences and these
paper bullets of the brain awe a man from the career of
his humour? No, the world must be peopled. When I
said I would die a bachelor, I did not think I should
live till I were married   235

Enter BEATRICE.

Here comes Beatrice. By this day, she's a fair lady! I do
spy some marks of love in her.

BEATRICE
Against my will I am sent to bid you come in
to dinner.

BENEDICK
Fair Beatrice, I thank you for your pains.   240

BEATRICE
I took no more pains for those thanks than you
take pains to thank me. If it had been painful I would
not have come.

BENEDICK
You take pleasure, then, in the message?

BEATRICE
Yea, just so much as you may take upon a   245
knife's point and choke a daw withal. You have no
stomach, signor? Fare you well.   *Exit.*

BENEDICK
Ha! 'Against my will I am sent to bid you come
in to dinner' – there's a double meaning in that. 'I took

sentences – *proverbs*

paper . . . brain – *feeble weapons of words*; awe – *frighten away*; career – *course*

humour – *desire*

I do spy . . . her – *(almost certainly a direction to the actress to show no such thing)*

pains – *effort*

Yea – *Yes* (Pron. yay); so much . . . withal – *(as a tame bird that chokes on a proffered morsel)*

daw – *jackdaw/raven*

stomach – *appetite*

no more pains for those thanks than you took pains to   250
thank me' – that's as much as to say, 'Any pains that I
take for you is as easy as thanks.' If I do not take pity of
her I am a villain; if I do not love her I am a Jew. I will
go get her picture.   *Exit.*

ACT 3, SCENE 1

Enter HERO and two gentlewomen,
MARGARET and URSULA.

HERO
    Good Margaret, run thee to the parlour;
    There shalt thou find my cousin Beatrice
    Proposing with the prince and Claudio;
    Whisper her ear and tell her I and Ursley
    Walk in the orchard, and our whole discourse   5
    Is all of her. Say that thou overheard'st us,
    And bid her steal into the pleachèd bower
    Where honeysuckles ripen'd by the sun
    Forbid the sun to enter, like favourites
    Made proud by princes that advance their pride   10
    Against that power that bred it; there will she hide her
    To listen our propose. This is thy office,
    Bear thee well in it, and leave us alone.

MARGARET
    I'll make her come, I warrant you, presently.

[Exit.]

HERO
    Now, Ursula, when Beatrice doth come,   15
    As we do trace this alley up and down

Jew – *an ungenerous spirit ('fool' makes a convenient substitute)*
get her picture – *find/commission a miniature portrait that could be carried on the person*

This whole scene is in VERSE.
Metre – line is short by 1 syl.
Be-a-**trice** (equiv. 3 syl.)

Proposing – *Conversing*
Ursley – *(names often appear in varied forms)*

steal – *creep*; pleachèd bower – *close-woven branched trees*

favourites – *preferred courtiers*   **fav**-ourites (equiv. 2 syl.)
Made . . . bred it – *challenge the authority of the one who raised them*
    Metre – 12 syl. line, probable anapest on 'will she **hide**' (see 'A Note on Metre')
our propose – *to our conversation*   Q – propose F – purpose

warrant – *guarantee*   -rant you **pres** (anapest – see 'A Note on Metre')

Be-a-**trice** (equiv. 3 syl.)

115

Our talk must only be of Benedick.
When I do name him, let it be thy part
To praise him more than ever man did merit;
My talk to thee must be how Benedick   20
Is sick in love with Beatrice. Of this matter
Is little Cupid's crafty arrow made,
That only wounds by hearsay.

Enter BEATRICE [who hides].

                              Now begin,
For look where Beatrice like a lapwing runs
Close by the ground to hear our conference.   25

URSULA [*to Hero*]
The pleasant'st angling is to see the fish
Cut with her golden oars the silver stream
And greedily devour the treacherous bait;
So angle we for Beatrice, who even now
Is couchèd in the woodbine coverture.   30
Fear you not my part of the dialogue.

HERO [*to Ursula*]
Then go we near her, that her ear lose nothing
Of the false sweet bait that we lay for it.
[*They approach Beatrice's hiding place.*]
– No, truly, Ursula, she is too disdainful.
I know her spirits are as coy and wild   35
As haggards of the rock.

URSULA   But are you sure
That Benedick loves Beatrice so entirely?

thy – *(Hero's use of thee and thy sets up the intimacy of the conversation* – see Intro.*)*

Bea-trice in this case equiv. 2 syl. It switches back and forth throughout the scene.

lapwing – *a small bird that nests on the ground, and so flies low*

                               con-fer-**ence** (equiv. 3 syl.)

                               pleas-ant'st (equiv. 2 syl.)

golden oars – *fins*

                               treacher-ous (equiv. 2 syl.)

                 -trice who **eve**- (anapest – see 'A Note on Metre')

couchèd – *hidden*; woodbine coverture – *bower of honeysuckle branches*

       Metre – headless line with an anapest on 'of the-**di**' (see 'A Note on Metre')

lose – *miss*

                               Urs-ula (equiv. 2 syl.)

coy – *evasive*

haggards – *untrained falcons (often used of wild women)*; rock – *cliff (blown by strong winds)*

HERO

So says the prince and my new-trothèd lord.

URSULA

And did they bid you tell her of it, madam?

HERO

They did entreat me to acquaint her of it;   40
But I persuaded them, if they lov'd Benedick,
To wish him wrestle with affection
And never to let Beatrice know of it.

URSULA

Why did you so? Doth not the gentleman
Deserve at full as fortunate a bed   45
As ever Beatrice shall couch upon?

HERO

O god of love! I know he doth deserve
As much as may be yielded to a man.
But Nature never fram'd a woman's heart
Of prouder stuff than that of Beatrice.   50
Disdain and Scorn ride sparkling in her eyes,
Misprising what they look on, and her wit
Values itself so highly that to her
All matter else seems weak. She cannot love,
Nor take no shape nor project of affection,   55
She is so self-endeared.

URSULA   Sure, I think so.
And therefore certainly it were not good
She knew his love, lest she'll make sport at it.

new-trothèd – *recently betrothed*

Metre – 12 syl. line
a-**ffec**-ti-**on** (equiv. 4 syl.)

Deserve . . . upon – *he fully deserves to sleep with a woman at least as good as Beatrice*
couch – *lie*

yielded – *offered/harvested (with connotations of a woman's yielding to sex)*

Disdain and Scorn – *allegorical figures* (see Intro.) **spark**-ling (equiv. 2 syl.)
Misprising – *Evaluating incorrectly*; wit – *intelligence*

All . . . weak – *Other qualities lack value*
take – *comprehend*; no . . . project – *no image (projection)*; affection – *love*

make sport – *jest*

HERO

> Why, you speak truth. I never yet saw man –
> How wise, how noble, young, how rarely featur'd – 60
> But she would spell him backward. If fair-faced,
> She would swear the gentleman should be her sister;
> If black, why Nature, drawing of an antic,
> Made a foul blot; if tall, a lance ill-headed;
> If low, an agate very vilely cut; 65
> If speaking, why, a vane blown with all winds;
> If silent, why, a block movèd with none.
> So turns she every man the wrong side out,
> And never gives to truth and virtue that
> Which simpleness and merit purchaseth. 70

URSULA

> Sure, sure, such carping is not commendable.

HERO

> No, not to be so odd and from all fashions
> As Beatrice is cannot be commendable.
> But who dare tell her so? If I should speak,
> She would mock me into air. O, she would laugh me 75
> Out of myself, press me to death with wit!
> Therefore let Benedick, like cover'd fire,
> Consume away in sighs, waste inwardly.
> It were a better death than die with mocks,
> Which is as bad as die with tickling. 80

URSULA

> Yet tell her of it; hear what she will say.

HERO

> No, rather I will go to Benedick
> And counsel him to fight against his passion.

How – *no matter how*; rarely – *finely*
spell him backward – *misrepresent him (as witches make spells)*
                         She would **swear** (anapest – see 'A Note on Metre')
antic – *clown*   F – antic Q – antique
foul blot – *(as of an error in writing with ink)*; ill-headed – *with a dull tip*
agate – *semi-precious stone*
vane – *weather vane*

never . . . purchaseth – *never gives credit where it is due, as honesty demands*

com-men-**da**-ble – Pron. differs from modern (emphasis on first syl.)

from all fashions – *distant from what is shared opinion*
No . . . commendable – *It is bad for Beatrice to stray so far from general agreement*

into air – *reduce me to nothing*   She would **mock** (anapest – see 'A Note on Metre')
press me to death – *punishment designed to extract a plea from a criminal*
cover'd fire – *smouldering*
sighs, waste – *lover's sighs were thought to use up heart's blood* (see: 1.2, pale)

                                 tick-l-**ing** (equiv. 3 syl.)

And truly, I'll devise some honest slanders
To stain my cousin with: one doth not know   85
How much an ill word may empoison liking.

URSULA

O, do not do your cousin such a wrong!
She cannot be so much without true judgement,
Having so swift and excellent a wit
As she is priz'd to have, as to refuse   90
So rare a gentleman as Signor Benedick.

HERO

He is the only man of Italy –
Always excepted my dear Claudio.

URSULA

I pray you, be not angry with me, madam,
Speaking my fancy. Signor Benedick,   95
For shape, for bearing, argument and valour,
Goes foremost in report through Italy.

HERO

Indeed, he hath an excellent good name.

URSULA

His excellence did earn it ere he had it.
When are you married, madam?   100

HERO

Why, every day, tomorrow! Come, go in,
I'll show thee some attires, and have thy counsel
Which is the best to furnish me tomorrow.

honest slanders – *criticisms that do not impinge on her virtue*

empoison – *poison, kill*

true – *sound*

priz'd – *reputed*
So rare – *Of such exceptional quality*   Metre – 12 syl. line

Always . . . Claudio – *(this is Hero's only line expressing her feelings for her fiancé)*

fancy – *thought*
argument – *reason or discourse*
Goes foremost in report – *Is placed first when talked about*

name – *reputation*

His . . . had it – *His worth pre-existed his reputation*
                      Metre – this line is short by 3 syl.

every day, tomorrow – *as of tomorrow, every day thereafter*
attires – *hair adornments*

URSULA [*to Hero*]

    She's limed, I warrant you! We have caught her,
    madam!

HERO [*to Ursula*]

    If it prove so, then loving goes by haps;   105
    Some Cupid kills with arrows, some with traps.

[Exeunt all but Beatrice.]

BEATRICE

    What fire is in mine ears? Can this be true?
    Stand I condemn'd for pride and scorn so much?
    Contempt, farewell; and maiden pride, adieu;
    No glory lives behind the back of such.   110
    And Benedick, love on, I will requite thee,
    Taming my wild heart to thy loving hand.
    If thou dost love, my kindness shall incite thee
    To bind our loves up in a holy band.
    For others say thou dost deserve, and I   115
    Believe it better than reportingly.   *Exit.*

ACT 3, SCENE 2

Enter DON PEDRO, CLAUDIO,
BENEDICK and LEONATO.

DON PEDRO

    I do but stay till your marriage be
    consummate, and then go I toward Aragon.

CLAUDIO

    I'll bring you thither, my lord, if you'll
    vouchsafe me.

limed – *caught by birdlime (ref. back to Beatrice as a lapwing)*   Q – limed F – tane

We have **caught** – anapest (see 'A Note on Metre')

haps – *chance*

The AB-plus-couplet rhyme form of this speech creates a mini-sonnet.

(10 rather than the usual 14 lines)

maiden pride – *pride in maintaining her virgin status*

lives . . . back – *waits on/attends*

holy band – *play on ring/bond (wedding rings were in use at this time, though not essential)*

better than reportingly – *she sees him as even more deserving than they say*

'I' and 'reportingly' probably rhymed in Elizabethan pronunciation

bring you thither – *accompany you there*

vouchsafe – *approve*

DON PEDRO

Nay, that would be as great a soil in the new 5
gloss of your marriage as to show a child his new coat
and forbid him to wear it. I will only be bold with
Benedick for his company, for from the crown of his
head to the sole of his foot, he is all mirth. He hath
twice or thrice cut Cupid's bowstring, and the little 10
hangman dare not shoot at him. He hath a heart as
sound as a bell, and his tongue is the clapper: for what
his heart thinks, his tongue speaks.

BENEDICK

Gallants, I am not as I have been.

LEONATO

So say I; methinks you are sadder. 15

CLAUDIO

I hope he be in love.

DON PEDRO

Hang him, truant! There's no true drop of
blood in him to be truly touched with love. If he be sad,
he wants money.

BENEDICK

I have the toothache. 20

DON PEDRO

Draw it.

BENEDICK

Hang it!

soil – *stain*

be bold with – *presume*

all mirth – *(no doubt a visual joke, with a newly sombre Benedick)*
twice . . . at him – *Benedick has disarmed love, until love fears to assail him*

clapper – *striking arm of a bell*

Gallants – *Gentlemen*

methinks – *it seems to me*

truant – *one who strays*

wants – *lacks*

toothache – *(traditionally associated with being in love)*

Draw it – *Pull it out*

Hang it – *Pull it out using a string*

CLAUDIO
You must hang it first and draw it afterwards.

DON PEDRO
What? Sigh for the toothache?

LEONATO
Where is but a humour or a worm.   25

BENEDICK
Well, everyone can master a grief but he that
has it.

CLAUDIO
Yet, say I, he is in love.

DON PEDRO
There is no appearance of fancy in him,
unless it be a fancy that he hath to strange disguises: as   30
to be a Dutchman today, a Frenchman tomorrow – [or
in the shape of two countries at once, as a German from
the waist downward, all slops, and a Spaniard from the
hip upward, no doublet.] Unless he have a fancy to this
foolery – as it appears he hath – he is no fool for   35
fancy, as you would have it appear he is.

CLAUDIO
If he be not in love with some woman there is
no believing old signs. 'A brushes his hat o'mornings:
what should that bode?

DON PEDRO
Hath any man seen him at the barber's?   40

hang ... afterwards – *hanging and then drawing of the entrails was the punishment for traitors*

humour ... worm – *rotten humours and worms were both offered as causes of toothache*

fancy – *love/ornament*
fancy – *whim*; strange disguises – *(Benedick has clearly updated his wardrobe)*
to be ... doublet – *(young Englishmen were mocked for adopting their fashions from all over)*
                                        Q – or ... doublet – passage absent in F
slops – *loose-fitting trousers*
no doublet – *(because a voluminous cloak covers his upper body)*

fancy – *at the end of the speech Don Pedro reverses the dual meanings of fancy from above*

'A – *He*; brushes his hat o'mornings – *(indicating a new fastidiousness)*
bode – *proclaim*

CLAUDIO

No, but the barber's man hath been seen with
him, and the old ornament of his cheek hath already
stuffed tennis balls.

LEONATO

Indeed, he looks younger than he did by the
loss of a beard.   45

DON PEDRO

Nay, 'a rubs himself with civet. Can you
smell him out by that?

CLAUDIO

That's as much as to say the sweet youth's in love.

DON PEDRO

The greatest note of it is his melancholy.

CLAUDIO

And when was he wont to wash his face?   50

DON PEDRO

Yea, or to paint himself? For the which I
hear what they say of him.

CLAUDIO

Nay, but his jesting spirit, which is now crept
into a lute-string and now governed by stops.

DON PEDRO

Indeed, that tells a heavy tale for him.   55
Conclude, conclude: he is in love.

old ornament . . . tennis balls – *(tennis balls were stuffed with hair)*

'a – *he*; civet – *a foppish perfume made from cat glands*

note – *marker*; melancholy – *lovers were traditionally so*

wont – *inclined* (Pron. wohnt)

paint – *use cosmetics*; For . . . him – *For this is what I have heard said of him*

stops – *frets/pauses (the lute was suitable for playing love songs)*

that . . . him – *we can read his weighty/serious story by this sign*

CLAUDIO

Nay, but I know who loves him.

DON PEDRO

That would I know too; I warrant one that
knows him not.

CLAUDIO

Yes, and his ill conditions, and in despite of all   60
dies for him.

DON PEDRO

She shall be buried with her face upwards.

BENEDICK

Yet is this no charm for the toothache. [*to
Leonato*] Old signor, walk aside with me. I have studied
eight or nine wise words to speak to you which these   65
hobby-horses must not hear.

[Exeunt Benedick and Leonato.]

DON PEDRO

For my life, to break with him about
Beatrice!

CLAUDIO

'Tis even so. Hero and Margaret have by this
played their parts with Beatrice, and then the two bears   70
will not bite one another when they meet.

Enter [DON] JOHN the bastard.

I warrant . . . not – *I bet it must be someone who doesn't know him properly*

ill conditions – *faults*
dies for him – *(connotations of orgasm)*

face upwards – *(underneath her man)*

hobby-horses – *tricksters*

For – *Upon*; break with – *negotiate*

by this – *it appears by this*
two . . . bite – *Prov.: now they have been matched they will cease to attack each other*

DON JOHN
　My lord and brother, God save you!

DON PEDRO
　Good e'en, brother.

DON JOHN
　If your leisure served, I would speak with you.

DON PEDRO
　In private?　　　　　　　　　　　　　　　　　75

DON JOHN
　If it please you; yet Count Claudio may hear,
　for what I would speak of concerns him.

DON PEDRO
　What's the matter?

DON JOHN
　[*to Claudio*] Means your lordship to be
　married tomorrow?　　　　　　　　　　　　　80

DON PEDRO
　You know he does.

DON JOHN
　I know not that when he knows what I know.

CLAUDIO
　If there be any impediment, I pray you discover
　it.

DON JOHN
　You may think I love you not. Let that appear　85

e'en – *evening*

leisure served – *if you have time*

.

discover – *reveal*

Let . . . manifest – *Let that be judged by my subsequent actions (heavily ironic, naturally)*

hereafter, and aim better at me by that I now will
manifest. For my brother – I think he holds you well and
in dearness of heart – hath holp to effect your ensuing
marriage; surely suit ill spent and labour ill bestowed.

DON PEDRO
Why, what's the matter?   90

DON JOHN
I came hither to tell you; and, circumstances
shortened – for she has been too long a-talking of – the
lady is disloyal.

CLAUDIO
Who, Hero?

DON JOHN
Even she: Leonato's Hero, your Hero, every   95
man's Hero.

CLAUDIO
Disloyal?

DON JOHN
The word is too good to paint out her
wickedness; I could say she were worse. Think you of a
worse title, and I will fit her to it. Wonder not till   100
further warrant. Go but with me, tonight you shall see
her chamber window entered, even the night before her
wedding day. If you love her then, tomorrow wed her.
But it would better fit your honour to change your mind.

CLAUDIO
May this be so?   105

aim better at me – *assess me more accurately*

hath holp – *has helped*

hither – *here*; circumstances shortened – *omitting the details, to be brief*

warrant – *evidence*

DON PEDRO
  I will not think it.

DON JOHN
  If you dare not trust that you see, confess not
  that you know. If you will follow me I will show you
  enough, and when you have seen more and heard more,
  proceed accordingly.   110

CLAUDIO
  If I see anything tonight why I should not
  marry her, tomorrow in the congregation where I
  should wed, there will I shame her.

DON PEDRO
  And as I wooed for thee to obtain her, I will
  join with thee to disgrace her.   115

DON JOHN
  I will disparage her no farther till you are my
  witnesses. Bear it coldly but till midnight, and let the
  issue show itself.

DON PEDRO
  O day untowardly turned!

CLAUDIO
  O mischief strangely thwarting!   120

DON JOHN
  O plague right well prevented! So will you say
  when you have seen the sequel.

[Exeunt.]

that – *what*; confess . . . know – *you may continue to refuse to admit the truth*

Bear it coldly – *Carry yourself without the heat of your anger/passion showing*

untowardly – *unfortunately*

strangely – *unexpectedly*

sequel – *what follows*

ACT 3, SCENE 3

Enter DOGBERRY[, the constable], and his compartner
[VERGES,] with the Watch[, among them
George SEACOAL and Hugh Oatcake].

DOGBERRY
Are you good men and true?

VERGES
Yea, or else it were pity but they should suffer
salvation, body and soul.

DOGBERRY
Nay, that were a punishment too good for
them, if they should have any allegiance in them, being   5
chosen for the prince's watch.

VERGES
Well, give them their charge, neighbour
Dogberry.

DOGBERRY
First, who think you the most desertless man
to be constable?   10

1 WATCHMAN
Hugh Oatcake, sir, or George Seacoal, for
they can write and read.

DOGBERRY
Come hither, neighbour Seacoal; [*Seacoal*
steps forward.] God hath blest you with a good name. To

compartner – *fellow office-bearer*

Notes to Dogberry and his assistants' habitual malapropisms will suggest the likely correct word.

salvation – *for damnation*

allegiance – *for disloyalty*

charge – *task*

desertless – *for deserving*

Oatcake and Seacoal – *(names suggesting provincial and therefore unsophisticated men)*

hither – *here*
good name – *(Seacoal was the superior grade of coal)*

be a well-favoured man is the gift of fortune, but to   15
write and read comes by nature.

SEACOAL
Both which, master constable –

DOGBERRY
You have. I knew it would be your answer.
Well, for your favour, sir, why, give God thanks, and
make no boast of it; and for your writing and reading,   20
let that appear when there is no need of such vanity.
You are thought here to be the most senseless and fit
man for the constable of the watch, therefore bear
you the lantern. [*Hands Seacoal the lantern.*] This is
your charge: you shall comprehend all vagrom men.   25
You are to bid any man stand, in the prince's name.

SEACOAL
How if 'a will not stand?

DOGBERRY
Why then, take no note of him, but let him
go, and presently call the rest of the watch together, and
thank God you are rid of a knave.   30

VERGES
If he will not stand when he is bidden, he is none
of the prince's subjects.

DOGBERRY
True, and they are to meddle with none but
the prince's subjects. You shall also make no noise in
the streets, for for the watch to babble and to talk is most   35
tolerable, and not to be endured.

well-favoured – *good looking*
comes by nature – *naturally (rather than by effort)*

SP – Bevington – Seacoal Q/F – Watch 2

favour – *face*

vanity – *(Dogberry may mean talents, or may be disparaging this kind of learning)*
senseless – *for sensible*

comprehend – *for apprehend*; vagrom – *for vagrant*

SP – Bevington – Seacoal Q/F – Watch 2

'a – *he*

knave – *rascal*

for for – *because for*
tolerable – *for intolerable*

WATCHMAN

We will rather sleep than talk; we know what
belongs to a watch.

DOGBERRY

Why, you speak like an ancient and most quiet
watchman. For I cannot see how sleeping should   40
offend. Only have a care that your bills be not stolen.
Well, you are to call at all the alehouses, and bid those
that are drunk get them to bed.

WATCHMAN

How if they will not?

DOGBERRY

Why then, let them alone till they are sober. If   45
they make you not then the better answer, you may say
they are not the men you took them for.

WATCHMAN

Well, sir.

DOGBERRY

If you meet a thief, you may suspect him, by
virtue of your office, to be no true man. And for such   50
kind of men, the less you meddle or make with them,
why, the more is for your honesty.

WATCHMAN

If we know him to be a thief, shall we not lay
hands on him?

DOGBERRY

Truly, by your office you may; but I think they   55

bills – *halberds (the weapon of the watch)*

Q – those F – them

If . . . for – *If they don't speak better when sobered up, you were mistaken in thinking them drunk*

by – *in accordance with*

that touch pitch will be defiled. The most peaceable
way for you, if you do take a thief, is to let him show
himself what he is, and steal out of your company.

VERGES
You have been always called a merciful man,
partner.   60

DOGBERRY
Truly, I would not hang a dog by my will,
much more a man who hath any honesty in him.

VERGES
If you hear a child cry in the night you must call
to the nurse and bid her still it.

WATCHMAN
How if the nurse be asleep and will not hear   65
us?

DOGBERRY
Why then, depart in peace, and let the child
wake her with crying; for the ewe that will not hear her
lamb when it baas will never answer a calf when he
bleats.   70

VERGES
'Tis very true.

DOGBERRY
This is the end of the charge. You, constable,
are to present the prince's own person. If you meet the
prince in the night you may stay him.

pitch – *black tar*; defiled – *contaminated* (Bib. Ecclesiastes 13.1)

take – *apprehend*

calf – *fool (the calf here is the watchman, a nurse is more likely to respond to the baby than him)*

charge – *duties they are charged with*

present – *represent*

stay – *stop/hold*

VERGES

Nay, by'r Lady, that I think 'a cannot.   75

DOGBERRY

Five shillings to one on't with any man that
knows the statutes. He may stay him – marry, not
without the prince be willing, for indeed the watch
ought to offend no man, and it is an offence to stay a
man against his will.   80

VERGES

By'r Lady, I think it be so.

DOGBERRY

Ha, ah ha! Well, masters, good night; an there
be any matter of weight chances, call up me. Keep your
fellows' counsels, and your own, and good night. [*to
Verges*] Come, neighbour. [*Dogberry and Verges begin to*   85
exit.]

SEACOAL

Well, masters, we hear our charge. Let us go sit
here upon the church bench till two, and then all to bed.

DOGBERRY

[*Returns.*] One word more, honest neighbours. I pray you watch about Signor Leonato's
door, for the wedding being there tomorrow, there is a   90
great coil tonight. Adieu. Be vigitant, I beseech you.

Exeunt [Dogberry and Verges].

by'r Lady – *by our Lady (Mary)*; 'a – *he*

on't – *on it (betting he is correct)*
statutes – *regulations*; marry – *indeed*

Ha, ah ha! – *(expressing pleasure at having scored a point by obtaining Verges' agreement)*
an there . . . chances – *if there happens to be anything important*
counsels – *private thoughts*

SP – Bevington – Seacoal Q/F – Watch

coil – *fuss*; vigitant – *for vigilant*

Enter BORACHIO *and* CONRADE.

BORACHIO
What, Conrade!

SEACOAL
[*aside*] Peace, stir not.

BORACHIO
Conrade, I say!

CONRADE
Here, man, I am at thy elbow.   95

BORACHIO
Mass, and my elbow itched; I thought there
would a scab follow!

CONRADE
I will owe thee an answer for that. And now,
forward with thy tale.

BORACHIO
Stand thee close, then, under this penthouse,   100
for it drizzles rain, and I will, like a true drunkard, utter
all to thee.

SEACOAL
[*aside*] Some treason, masters. Yet stand close.

BORACHIO
Therefore, know I have earned of Don John a
thousand ducats.   105

SP – Capell – Seacoal Q/F – Watch

Mass – *By the mass (used as an expletive)*

penthouse – *overhanging enclosed balcony*
true drunkard – *(for in vino veritas)*

CONRADE
Is it possible that any villainy should be so
dear?

BORACHIO
Thou shouldst rather ask if it were possible
any villainy should be so rich. For when rich villains
have need of poor ones, poor ones may make what price   110
they will.

CONRADE
I wonder at it.

BORACHIO
That shows thou art unconfirmed. Thou
knowest that the fashion of a doublet, or a hat, or a
cloak, is nothing to a man.   115

CONRADE
Yes, it is apparel.

BORACHIO
I mean the fashion.

CONRADE
Yes, the fashion is the fashion.

BORACHIO
Tush, I may as well say the fool's the fool. But
seest thou not what a deformed thief this fashion is?   120

WATCHMAN
[*aside*] I know that Deformed. 'A has been
a vile thief this seven year; 'a goes up and down like a
gentleman; I remember his name.

dear – *valuable*

unconfirmed – *ignorant*

is nothing to a man – *says nothing about what kind of man he is*

Tush – *(dismissive expletive)*
deformed – *malforming, disguising*

Deformed – *(the watchman thinks Borachio is speaking of a person)*; 'A – *He*
'a goes ... down – *he parades himself*

BORACHIO
Didst thou not hear somebody?

CONRADE
No, 'twas the vane on the house.   125

BORACHIO
Seest thou not, I say, what a deformed thief
this fashion is, how giddily 'a turns about all the
hot-bloods between fourteen and five-and-thirty,
sometimes fashioning them like Pharaoh's soldiers in
the reechy painting, sometime like god Bel's priests in   130
the old church window, sometime like the shaven
Hercules in the smirched worm-eaten tapestry, where
his codpiece seems as massy as his club.

CONRADE
All this I see, and I see that the fashion wears
out more apparel than the man. But art not thou thyself 135
giddy with the fashion, too, that thou hast shifted out of
thy tale into telling me of the fashion?

BORACHIO
Not so neither. But know that I have tonight
wooed Margaret, the Lady Hero's gentlewoman, by the
name of Hero; she leans me out at her mistress'   140
chamber window, bids me a thousand times goodnight
– I tell this tale vilely. I should first tell thee how the
prince, Claudio and my master, planted and placed and
possessed by my master Don John, saw afar off in the
orchard this amiable encounter.   145

CONRADE
And thought they Margaret was Hero?

vane – *i.e. weathervane blowing around*

Seest thou not – *Don't you see*
'a – *he*

sometimes . . . club – *all his examples suggest dated, old-fashioned garb*; fashioning – *shaping*; reechy – *smokey (dark with smoke)*; Bel's priests – *the priests of Baal* (Bib. Apocrypha); church window – *(of bright coloured glass)*; shaven – *conflating Hercules with Samson* (Bib.); Hercules – (see Myth); codpiece – *prominent fabric pouch worn at the front of pantaloons*; massy – *huge*

fashion . . . apparel – *clothes are replaced on whim more than due to use*   Q – and I F – and

giddy – *changeable*; shifted out – *pun on changing clothes/strayed away from his point*

Not so neither – *(he is about to come to the point)*

vilely – *badly*

possessed – *informed*

BORACHIO

Two of them did, the prince and Claudio,
but the devil my master knew she was Margaret. And
partly by his oaths, which first possessed them, partly
by the dark night, which did deceive them, but chiefly   150
by my villainy, which did confirm any slander that Don
John had made, away went Claudio enraged, swore he
would meet her as he was appointed next morning at
the temple, and there, before the whole congregation,
shame her with what he saw o'ernight, and send her   155
home again without a husband.

1 WATCHMAN

[*Starts out upon them.*] We charge you in
the prince's name, stand!

SEACOAL

Call up the right master constable! We have
here recovered the most dangerous piece of lechery   160
that ever was known in the commonwealth!

1 WATCHMAN

And one Deformed is one of them. I know
him, 'a wears a lock.

CONRADE

Masters, masters –

SEACOAL

You'll be made bring Deformed forth, I   165
warrant you.

CONRADE

Masters –

o'ernight – *overnight*

Q/F – alternate Watch 1, Watch 2 for remainder of scene

recovered – *for discovered*; lechery – *for treachery*

one Deformed – *(still imagining Deformed to be a person)*
'a – *he*; a lock – *a foppish fashion of growing a single lock of hair longer than the others*

You'll . . . forth – *You will be forced to present your associate, Deformed*
warrant – *guarantee*

SEACOAL

Never speak, we charge you! Let us obey you
to go with us.

BORACHIO

[*to Conrade*] We are like to prove a goodly
commodity, being taken up of these men's bills.

170

CONRADE

A commodity in question, I warrant you.
Come, we'll obey you.

Exeunt.

ACT 3, SCENE 4

Enter HERO, MARGARET and URSULA.

HERO

Good Ursula, wake my cousin Beatrice and desire
her to rise.

URSULA

I will, lady.

HERO

And bid her come hither.

URSULA

Well.   [*Exit.*]   5

MARGARET

Troth, I think your other rebato were better.

obey – *for oblige or compel*

goodly commodity – *valuable tradeables/goods on credit*
taken up – *received on credit/collected/arrested*; of – *by*; bills – *halberds/promisary notes*

in question – *subject to inquiry or legal proceedings*

hither – *here*

Troth – *In truth*; rebato – *wired linen collar*

HERO

No, pray thee, good Meg, I'll wear this.

MARGARET

By my troth, 's not so good, and I warrant
your cousin will say so.

HERO

My cousin's a fool, and thou art another. I'll wear   10
none but this.

MARGARET

I like the new tire within excellently, if the
hair were a thought browner. And your gown's a most
rare fashion, i'faith. I saw the Duchess of Milan's gown
that they praise so.   15

HERO

O, that exceeds, they say.

MARGARET

By my troth, 's but a night-gown in respect of
yours – cloth o'gold, and cuts, and laced with silver, set
with pearls, down sleeves, side sleeves and skirts round
underborne with a bluish tinsel. But for a fine, quaint,   20
graceful and excellent fashion, yours is worth ten on't.

HERO

God give me joy to wear it, for my heart is
exceeding heavy.

MARGARET

'Twill be heavier soon by the weight of a
man.   25

warrant – *wager*

tire – *hair decoration made with wire, charms and extra hair*
a thought browner – *the hair on the tire is a little too light to match Hero's dark hair*
rare fashion – *fine style*; i'faith – *in faith (truthfully)*

exceeds – *exceeds other examples/praise*

night-gown – *more a dressing gown than a nightdress*
cloth o'gold – *(wedding gowns were not white in this period)*; cuts – *slashes in the fabric*
down sleeves – *fastened at the wrist*; side sleeves – *hanging loose from the shoulder*
underborne – *on the exposed petticoat*; quaint – *dainty*
cloth . . . tinsel – *all typical features of Elizabethan noblewomen's dress*; on't – *of it*

heavy – *presumably meaning apprehensive here*

HERO

Fie upon thee! Art not ashamed?

MARGARET

Of what, lady? Of speaking honourably? Is
not marriage honourable in a beggar? Is not your lord
honourable without marriage? I think you would have
me say, saving your reverence, 'a husband'. An bad   30
thinking do not wrest true speaking, I'll offend nobody.
Is there any harm in 'the heavier for a husband'? None,
I think, an it be the right husband and the right wife;
otherwise 'tis light and not heavy.

Enter BEATRICE.

Ask my lady Beatrice else; here she comes.   35

HERO

Good morrow, coz.

BEATRICE

Good morrow, sweet Hero.

HERO

Why, how now? Do you speak in the sick tune?

BEATRICE

I am out of all other tune, methinks.

MARGARET

Clap's into 'Light o'love', that goes without   40
a burden. Do you sing it, and I'll dance it.

Fie – *(a serious reprimand)*; Art – *Are you*

in a beggar – *i.e. even in*

saving your reverence – *at the risk of offending*; An – *If*
wrest – *warp*; bad . . . speaking – *(Margaret blames Hero's dirty mind for twisting her words)*
an . . . wife – *i.e. if they are married (or suited?) to each other*
light – *faithless*

else – *otherwise*

coz – *cousin*

Good . . . Hero – *(Beatrice must speak as if with a cold for Hero's response to make sense)*

methinks – *it seems*

Clap's – *Clap us (Lead us into)*; 'Light o'love' – *a popular song*; goes without – *doesn't*
burden – *low (male) accompaniment/weight*   *require*

BEATRICE

Ye light o'love with your heels? Then if your
husband have stables enough, you'll see he shall lack
no barns.

MARGARET

O illegitimate construction! I scorn that with   45
my heels.

BEATRICE

'Tis almost five o'clock, cousin; 'tis time you
were ready. By my troth, I am exceeding ill. Hey-ho!

MARGARET

For a hawk, a horse, or a husband?

BEATRICE

For the letter that begins them all: H.   50

MARGARET

Well, an you be not turned Turk, there's no
more sailing by the star.

BEATRICE

What means the fool, trow?

MARGARET

Nothing, I, but God send everyone their
heart's desire.   55

HERO

These gloves the count sent me, they are an
excellent perfume.

Ye – *You are*; heels – *(to dance is to kick up heels, but light heels means unchaste)*
stables enough – *plenty of rooms*; see – *ensure*   Q – see F – look
barns – *pun on bairns (babies)*

illegitimate construction – *false conclusion/bastard babies*
scorn . . . heels – *ref. to the backwards kick of a horse (reflecting Beatrice's line above)*

By my troth – *Truthfully*

hawk . . . husband – *Prov. a ballad 'hey-ho for a husband'* (see 2.1)

H – *punning on ache (but can be played as a sneeze)*

an you – *if Beatrice*; turned Turk – *Prov.: has forsaken her faith*
no more . . . star – *even the North star cannot be trusted to stay firm for navigation*

trow – *I wonder*

gloves – *(common lovers' gifts, with expensive ones often perfumed)*

BEATRICE
  I am stuffed, cousin, I cannot smell.

MARGARET
  A maid and stuffed! There's goodly catching
  of cold.   60

BEATRICE
  O God help me, God help me, how long have
  you professed apprehension?

MARGARET
  Ever since you left it. Doth not my wit
  become me rarely?

BEATRICE
  It is not seen enough; you should wear it in   65
  your cap. By my troth, I am sick.

MARGARET
  Get you some of this distilled carduus
  benedictus, and lay it to your heart; it is the only thing
  for a qualm.

HERO
  There thou prick'st her with a thistle.   70

BEATRICE
  Benedictus? Why benedictus? You have some
  moral in this benedictus.

MARGARET
  Moral? No, by my troth, I have no moral
  meaning, I meant plain holy-thistle. You may think

stuffed – *i.e. her nose is stuffed up from her cold*

stuffed – *pregnant*

professed apprehension – *made claims to wit*

Ever since you left it – *(Margaret is taking over Beatrice's role)*
become me rarely – *suit me finely*

not seen enough – *(play on rarely – infrequently)*
wear it in you cap – *(as a fool's coxcomb/where men put an object to signify their allegiance)*

lay . . . heart – *bind it to your chest for medicinal purposes (with clear other meaning)*
qualm – *tremor or faintness (connotations of orgasm are in play)*

thistle – *the benedictus herb was a kind of thistle, called 'holy' or 'blessed'*

moral – *lesson*

holy-thistle – *see above*

perchance that I think you are in love? Nay, by'r Lady, I   75
am not such a fool to think what I list, nor I list not to
think what I can, nor indeed I cannot think, if I would
think my heart out of thinking, that you are in love, or
that you will be in love, or that you can be in love. Yet
Benedick was such another, and now is he become a   80
man. He swore he would never marry, and yet now in
despite of his heart he eats his meat without grudging.
And how you may be converted I know not, but
methinks you look with your eyes as other women do.

BEATRICE
What pace is this that thy tongue keeps?   85

MARGARET
Not a false gallop.

Enter URSULA.

URSULA
Madam, withdraw! The prince, the count,
Signor Benedick, Don John and all the gallants of the
town are come to fetch you to church.

HERO
Help to dress me, good coz, good Meg, good   90
Ursula.

[Exeunt.]

Nay – *No*
list – *please*

think . . . thinking – *i.e. she would never think something so extreme/outrageous*

such another – *another who rejects love*

eats his meat – *accepts his human appetites*

methinks – *it seems to me*

false gallop – *fast canter instead of a gallop's authentic stride (i.e. her claims are genuine)*

withdraw – *(Hero is not yet dressed to receive outsiders)*
gallants – *gentlemen*

ACT 3, SCENE 5

Enter LEONATO, [DOGBERRY,] the constable,
and [VERGES,] the headborough.

LEONATO

What would you with me, honest neighbour?

DOGBERRY

Marry, sir, I would have some confidence
with you, that discerns you nearly.

LEONATO

Brief, I pray you, for you see it is a busy time
with me.   5

DOGBERRY

Marry, this it is, sir.

VERGES

Yes, in truth it is, sir.

LEONATO

What is it, my good friends?

DOGBERRY

Goodman Verges, sir, speaks a little off the
matter. An old man, sir, and his wits are not so blunt as,   10
God help, I would desire they were; but, in faith, honest
as the skin between his brows.

VERGES

Yes, I thank God, I am as honest as any man
living, that is an old man and no honester than I.

headborough – *parish officer*

Marry – *Indeed*; confidence – *for conference*
discerns – *for concerns*

off the matter – *off topic*
blunt – *for sharp*

DOGBERRY

Comparisons are odorous; palabras, neighbour   15
Verges.

LEONATO

Neighbours, you are tedious.

DOGBERRY

It pleases your worship to say so, but we are
the poor duke's officers. But truly, for mine own part, if
I were as tedious as a king I could find in my heart to   20
bestow it all of your worship.

LEONATO

All thy tediousness on me, ah?

DOGBERRY

Yea, an 'twere a thousand pound more than
'tis, for I hear as good exclamation on your worship as
of any man in the city, and though I be but a poor man, 25
I am glad to hear it.

VERGES

And so am I.

LEONATO

I would fain know what you have to say.

VERGES

Marry, sir, our watch tonight, excepting your
worship's presence, ha' ta'en a couple of as arrant   30
knaves as any in Messina.

DOGBERRY

A good old man, sir, he will be talking. As they

odorous – *for odious* (Prov.); palabras – *silence*

tedious – *taking too long*

Dogberry takes tedious to mean affluent-looking.

an . . . 'tis – *if his fortune (tediousness) were that much greater*   Q – pound F – times
exclamation – *for commendation*

fain – *gladly*

ha' ta'en – *has taken*; arrant – *thorough*

say, 'When the age is in, the wit is out.' God help us, it
is a world to see! Well said, i'faith, neighbour Verges.
Well, God's a good man. An two men ride of a horse, 35
one must ride behind. An honest soul, i'faith, sir,
by my troth, he is, as ever broke bread. But, God is
to be worshipped, all men are not alike. Alas, good
neighbour!

LEONATO
Indeed, neighbour, he comes too short of you. 40

DOGBERRY
Gifts that God gives.

LEONATO
I must leave you.

DOGBERRY
One word, sir. Our watch, sir, have indeed
comprehended two aspicious persons, and we would
have them this morning examined before your worship. 45

LEONATO
Take their examination yourself, and bring it
me. I am now in great haste, as it may appear unto you.

DOGBERRY
It shall be suffigance.

LEONATO
Drink some wine ere you go. Fare you well!

[Enter Messenger.]

a world to see – *Verges' foolishness is a sight worth seeing*; i'faith – *in faith (truthfully)*
An . . . horse – *If two men ride a horse together*

by my troth – *truthfully*

he . . . you – *above Dogberry complained that Verges talks too much, Leonato points out that he talks less than Dogberry, though he knows Dogberry will take his comment to refer to Verges' lesser qualities. May also include a joke about the actors' relative heights.*

comprehended – *for apprehended*; aspicious – *for suspicious*

suffigance – *for sufficient*

ere – *before*

MESSENGER

My lord, they stay for you to give your   50
daughter to her husband.

LEONATO

I'll wait upon them; I am ready.

[Exit with Messenger.]

DOGBERRY

Go, good partner, go get you to Francis
Seacoal. Bid him bring his pen and inkhorn to the jail;
we are now to examination these men.   55

VERGES

And we must do it wisely.

DOGBERRY

We will spare for no wit, I warrant you. Here's
that shall drive some of them to a noncome. Only get
the learned writer to set down our excommunication,
and meet me at the jail   60

[Exeunt.]

ACT 4, SCENE 1

Enter DON PEDRO, [DON JOHN the] bastard,
LEONATO, FRIAR [Francis], CLAUDIO, BENEDICK,
HERO and BEATRICE [, with others].

LEONATO

Come, Friar Francis, be brief: only to the plain
form of marriage, and you shall recount their particular
duties afterwards.

stay – *wait*

wait upon – *attend*

Francis Seacoal – *could be the name of the Sexton, or an error conflating George with the Friar*

Q – examination these F – examine those

warrant – *guarantee*
noncome – *probably for being nonplussed (perplexed)*
excommunication – *for communication*

plain form – *(all that was required for marriage was a mutual declaration by the couple)*
recount . . . afterwards – *(but the minister might say more, if he wished)*

FRIAR
You come hither, my lord, to marry this lady?

CLAUDIO
No.   5

LEONATO
To be married to her, Friar; you come to marry
her.

FRIAR
Lady, you come hither to be married to this count?

HERO
I do.

FRIAR
If either of you know any inward impediment why   10
you should not be conjoined, I charge you on your souls
to utter it.

CLAUDIO
Know you any, Hero?

HERO
None, my lord.

FRIAR
Know you any, Count?   15

LEONATO
I dare make his answer: none.

hither – *here*

To . . . her – *(an awkward pause seems called for preceding Leonato's line)*

inward – *known to themselves*
conjoined – *married*; charge – *demand*

CLAUDIO

O, what men dare do! What men may do! What
men daily do, not knowing what they do!

BENEDICK

How now? Interjections? Why then, some be
of laughing, as ha, ha, he.   20

CLAUDIO

Stand thee by, Friar. [*to Leonato*] Father, by your leave:
Will you with free and unconstrainèd soul
Give me this maid, your daughter?

LEONATO

As freely, son, as God did give her me.

CLAUDIO

And what have I to give you back whose worth   25
May counterpoise this rich and precious gift?

DON PEDRO

Nothing, unless you render her again.

CLAUDIO

Sweet Prince, you learn me noble thankfulness.
There, Leonato, take her back again.
Give not this rotten orange to your friend;   30
She's but the sign and semblance of her honour.
Behold how like a maid she blushes here!
O, what authority and show of truth
Can cunning sin cover itself withal!
Comes not that blood as modest evidence   35
To witness simple virtue? Would you not swear,
All you that see her, that she were a maid,

Interjections? . . . ha, ha, he – *quotation playing on rhetorical forms (so not as silly as he sounds)* Source: William Lyly, *Short Introduction of Latin Grammar*

Stand thee by – *Stand aside* The scene moves from PROSE to VERSE until
unconstrainèd – *without reserve* line 254.
Metre – this line is short by 3 syl.

counterpoise – *weigh equally*

render – *return*

learn – *teach*

rotten orange – *i.e. with perfect skin concealing internal decay*
semblance – *representation* **sem**-blance (equiv. 2 sy.)
maid – *virgin*

cover – *conceal*
Comes . . . virtue – *Would you not think her blush signified straightforward innocence*
-tue? Would **you** (anapest – see 'A Note on Metre')

By these exterior shows? But she is none;
She knows the heat of a luxurious bed.
Her blush is guiltiness, not modesty.   40

LEONATO
What do you mean, my lord?

CLAUDIO
Not to be married, not to knit my soul
To an approvèd wanton.

LEONATO
Dear my lord, if you, in your own proof,
Have vanquish'd the resistance of her youth   45
And made defeat of her virginity –

CLAUDIO
I know what you would say: if I have known her,
You will say she did embrace me as a husband
And so extenuate the forehand sin.
No, Leonato,   50
I never tempted her with word too large,
But as a brother to his sister show'd
Bashful sincerity and comely love.

HERO
And seem'd I ever otherwise to you?

CLAUDIO
Out on thee, seeming! I will write against it: 55
You seem to me as Dian in her orb,
As chaste as is the bud ere it be blown;
But you are more intemperate in your blood

ex-**ter**-ior (equiv. 3 syl.)

luxurious – *lustful*   lux-**u**-rious (equiv. 3 syl.)

Metre – this line is short by 4 syl.

Claudio miscasts Leonato's 'mean' as intend to do, rather than imply.

approvèd wanton – *proven harlot*   Metre – line is short by 3 syl.

you . . . proof – *if you made trial of her yourself*   Headless line (see 'A Note on Metre')

known her – *had sex with her*

You will **say** (anapest – see 'A Note on Metre')

extenuate . . . sin – *(the sin of sex before marriage would not apply)*

Metre – line is short by 5 syl.

word too large – *too forward a proposition*

bashful . . . love – *modest praise and decorous love*

Out on thee – *Curses on you*; write against it – *publish its faults*

Dian in her orb – *goddess of chastity in the moon* (see Myth)

bud . . . blown – *bud of a flower before it blooms ('blown' also suggests rotten)*

intemperate – *unmoderated*   in-**temp**-erate (equiv. 3 syl.)

Than Venus, or those pamper'd animals
That rage in savage sensuality.   60

HERO
Is my lord well that he doth speak so wide?

LEONATO [*to Don Pedro*]
Sweet Prince, why speak not you?

DON PEDRO   What should I speak?
I stand dishonour'd that have gone about
To link my dear friend to a common stale.

LEONATO
Are these things spoken, or do I but dream?   65

DON JOHN
Sir, they are spoken, and these things are true.

BENEDICK
This looks not like a nuptial.

HERO   True? O God!

CLAUDIO   Leonato, stand I here?
Is this the prince? Is this the prince's brother?
Is this face Hero's? Are our eyes our own?

LEONATO
All this is so, but what of this, my lord?   70

CLAUDIO
Let me but move one question to your daughter,

pamper'd animals – *indulged pets*
rage in savage sensuality – *lust without constraint*

wide – *wide of the mark*

common stale – *lowest degree of prostitute*

Metre – Ambiguous three-line structure – see Series Introduction

move – *put*

And by that fatherly and kindly power
That you have in her bid her answer truly.

LEONATO
I charge thee do so, as thou art my child.

HERO
O, God defend me, how am I beset!   75
What kind of catechizing call you this?

CLAUDIO
To make you answer truly to your name.

HERO
Is it not Hero? Who can blot that name
With any just reproach?

CLAUDIO   Marry, that can Hero;
Hero itself can blot out Hero's virtue.   80
What man was he talk'd with you yesternight
Out at your window betwixt twelve and one?
Now, if you are a maid, answer to this.

HERO
I talk'd with no man at that hour, my lord.

DON PEDRO
Why, then are you no maiden. Leonato,   85
I am sorry you must hear. Upon mine honour,
Myself, my brother and this grievèd count
Did see her, hear her, at that hour last night,
Talk with a ruffian at her chamber window,
Who hath indeed, most like a liberal villain,   90

beset – *set upon*
catechizing – *a series of questions designed to determine religious faith*

Traditionally the first question of the catechism is 'What is your name?'

Marry – *Indeed*   Metre – Marry (equiv. 1 syl.) or indicating an overlap with Hero's line
Hero . . . virtue – *ref. to Greek mythology* (see Myth) *(this Hero wipes out her namesake's virtue)*

Q – are you F – you are
I am **so**- (anapest – see 'A Note on Metre')

ruff-ian (equiv. 2 syl.)

liberal – *free with what he gives out*

Confess'd the vile encounters they have had
A thousand times in secret.

DON JOHN

Fie, fie, they are not to be named, my lord,
Not to be spoke of!
There is not chastity enough in language   95
Without offence to utter them. Thus, pretty lady,
I am sorry for thy much misgovernment.

CLAUDIO

O Hero! What a Hero hadst thou been
If half thy outward graces had been plac'd
About thy thoughts and counsels of thy heart!   100
But fare thee well, most foul, most fair. Farewell
Thou pure impiety and impious purity.
For thee I'll lock up all the gates of love,
And on my eyelids shall conjecture hang
To turn all beauty into thoughts of harm,   105
And never shall it more be gracious.

LEONATO

Hath no man's dagger here a point for me?
[*Hero falls.*]

BEATRICE

Why, how now, cousin! Wherefore sink you down?

DON JOHN

Come, let us go; these things come thus to light
Smother her spirits up.

[*Exeunt Don Pedro, Claudio and Don John.*]

Metre – this line is short by 3 syl.

Fie – *Shame*

Metre – line is short by 5 syl.; Q – spoke F – spoken

There . . . them – *there is no decorous way to describe her acts*

Metre – irregular line of 13 syl.

much misgovernment – *great lack of control*   I am **so**- (anapest – see 'A Note on Metre')

outward graces – *admirable appearance*

thy thoughts – *(can be amended to the)*

imp-ious (equiv. 2 syl.); 12 syl. line

all . . . love – *the senses, whereby love was supposed to enter the body*

conjecture – *presumption of ill*

it – *i.e. beauty*   **grac**-i-**ous** (equiv. 3 syl.)

Wherefore – *Why*

spirits – *life force (it seems John already suspects she may be dying)*

BENEDICK   How doth the lady?

BEATRICE   Dead, I think. Help, uncle!   110
Hero! Why Hero! Uncle, Signor Benedick, Friar!

LEONATO
O Fate, take not away thy heavy hand!
Death is the fairest cover for her shame
That may be wish'd for.

BEATRICE
How now, cousin Hero?   115
[*Hero stirs.*]

FRIAR
Have comfort, lady.

LEONATO
Dost thou look up?

FRIAR
Yea, wherefore should she not?

LEONATO
Wherefore? Why, doth not every earthly thing
Cry shame upon her? Could she here deny   120
The story that is printed in her blood?
Do not live, Hero; do not ope thine eyes!
For did I think thou wouldst not quickly die,
Thought I thy spirits were stronger than thy shames,
Myself would on the rearward of reproaches   125
Strike at thy life. Griev'd I, I had but one?
Chid I for that at frugal Nature's frame?

Metre – Ambiguous three-line structure – see Series Introduction

Dead, I think – *(Claudio and Don Pedro may hear this as they exit)*

Metre – Irregular line of 14 syl.

take . . . hand – *expressing hope that she has indeed fallen dead*

Metre – That . . . not – this sequence of five short lines from three speakers is metrically ambiguous

wherefore – *why*

printed in her blood – *(Leonato, too, takes her blush to signify guiltiness)*
ope – *open*

Thought I – *If I thought*; spirits – *spirit to live*; shames – *(which should kill her)*
Myself . . . life – *he will become the rear (follow-up) guard and kill her himself*
but one – *only one child*
Chid . . . frame – *Rebuked Nature for being ungenerous*

O, one too much by thee! Why had I one?
Why ever wast thou lovely in my eyes?
Why had I not with charitable hand   130
Took up a beggar's issue at my gates,
Who smirchèd thus, and mir'd with infamy,
I might have said: 'No part of it is mine;
This shame derives itself from unknown loins.'
But mine, and mine I lov'd, and mine I prais'd,   135
And mine that I was proud on – mine so much
That I myself was to myself not mine
Valuing of her. Why she – O, she is fallen
Into a pit of ink that the wide sea
Hath drops too few to wash her clean again,   140
And salt too little which may season give
To her foul-tainted flesh.

BENEDICK   Sir, sir, be patient.
For my part, I am so attired in wonder
I know not what to say.

BEATRICE
O, on my soul, my cousin is belied!   145

BENEDICK
Lady, were you her bedfellow last night?

BEATRICE
No, truly, not – although until last night
I have this twelvemonth been her bedfellow.

LEONATO
Confirm'd, confirm'd! O, that is stronger made
Which was before barred up with ribs of iron.   150
Would the two princes lie, and Claudio lie

Took . . . issue – *Adopted a beggar's child*

mir'd with infamy – *muddied with ignoble origins*   Q – smirched F – smeered

That . . . mine – *I cared nothing for myself*

    Metre – 12 syl. line. Can be scanned with '**Val**-u-ing' as a dactyl (see 'A Note on Metre')

salt . . . flesh – *(brine was used to preserve meat, but could also cover the taste of decay)*

attired – *cloaked/clothed*; wonder – *astonishment*

    Metre – line is short by 4 syl.

belied – *lied against*

bedfellow – *(beds were shared routinely in this period)*

that – *that thing (the accusation)*

barred up – *reinforced*

Who lov'd her so, that speaking of her foulness
Wash'd it with tears? Hence from her, let her die.

FRIAR
Hear me a little:
For I have only been silent so long,   155
And given way unto this course of fortune,
By noting of the lady. I have mark'd
A thousand blushing apparitions
To start into her face, a thousand innocent shames
In angel whiteness beat away those blushes;   160
And in her eye there hath appear'd a fire
To burn the errors that these princes hold
Against her maiden truth. Call me a fool,
Trust not my reading nor my observations,
Which with experimental seal doth warrant   165
The tenor of my book; trust not my age,
My reverence, calling nor divinity,
If this sweet lady lie not guiltless here
Under some biting error.

LEONATO   Friar, it cannot be.
Thou seest that all the grace that she hath left   170
Is that she will not add to her damnation
A sin of perjury. She not denies it.
Why seek'st thou then to cover with excuse
That which appears in proper nakedness

FRIAR
Lady, what man is he you are accus'd of?   175

HERO
They know that do accuse me. I know none.
If I know more of any man alive

Hence from her – *Away with her*

Metre – line is short by 5 syl.

given . . . fortune – *allowed matters to go on this way*
noting of – *observing*

app-ar-**it**-i-**ons** (equiv. 5 syl.)
Metre – irregular 12 syl. line
Q – beat F – beare

Which . . . book – *his experience has confirmed what he learned from books*

rev-erence (equiv. 2 syl.)

Metre – if shared, this line is 12 syl.

proper nakedness – *appropriately uncovered*

Than that which maiden modesty doth warrant,
Let all my sins lack mercy! – O my father,
Prove you that any man with me convers'd   180
At hours unmeet, or that I yesternight
Maintain'd the change of words with any creature,
Refuse me, hate me, torture me to death!

FRIAR
There is some strange misprision in the princes.

BENEDICK
Two of them have the very bent of honour.   185
And if their wisdoms be misled in this,
The practice of it lives in John the bastard,
Whose spirits toil in frame of villainies.

LEONATO
I know not. If they speak but truth of her,
These hands shall tear her; if they wrong her honour,   190
The proudest of them shall well hear of it.
Time hath not yet so dried this blood of mine,
Nor age so eat up my invention,
Nor fortune made such havoc of my means,
Nor my bad life reft me so much of friends   195
But they shall find awak'd in such a kind
Both strength of limb and policy of mind,
Ability in means and choice of friends
To quit me of them throughly.

FRIAR   Pause awhile
And let my counsel sway you in this case.   200
Your daughter here the princes left for dead.
Let her awhile be secretly kept in,
And publish it that she is dead indeed.

warrant – *authorize*

unmeet – *inappropriate*
Maintain'd ... words – *Conversed*
Refuse – *Refuse to acknowledge/Disown*

misprision – *misapprehension*

very bent – *complete inclination to*

bastard – *(first time his illegitimacy is mentioned)*
Whose ... frame of – *Whose energy works to create*

well hear of it – *be challenged*

invention – *thinking ability*   in-**ven**-ti-**on** (equiv. 4 syl.)
fortune ... means – *fate has not diminished his wealth*
reft – *bereft*

quit ... throughly – *settle the score with them*

Maintain a mourning ostentation,
And on your family's old monument   205
Hang mournful epitaphs, and do all rites
That appertain unto a burial.

LEONATO
What shall become of this? What will this do?

FRIAR
Marry, this well carri'd shall on her behalf
Change slander to remorse; that is some good.   210
But not for that dream I on this strange course,
But on this travail look for greater birth:
She, dying, as it must be so maintain'd,
Upon the instant that she was accus'd,
Shall be lamented, piti'd and excus'd   215
Of every hearer. For it so falls out
That what we have we prize not to the worth
Whiles we enjoy it, but being lack'd and lost,
Why, then we rack the value, then we find
The virtue that possession would not show us   220
Whiles it was ours. So will it fare with Claudio:
When he shall hear she died upon his words,
Th'idea of her life shall sweetly creep
Into his study of imagination,
And every lovely organ of her life   225
Shall come apparell'd in more precious habit,
More moving, delicate and full of life,
Into the eye and prospect of his soul
Than when she liv'd indeed. Then shall he mourn –
If ever love had interest in his liver –   230
And wish he had not so accusèd her;
No, though he thought his accusation true.
Let this be so, and doubt not but success

mourning ostentation – *formal displays of mourning*   **ost**-en-**ta**-ti-**on** (equiv. 5 syl.)
monument – *tomb*

become – *come from*

Marry – *Indeed*; well carried – *done properly*   Ma-rry, **this** (anapest – see 'A Note on
Metre')

travail – *work/trials*; greater birth – *better things to come out of it*
so maintain'd – *claimed*

Of – *By*

it, but **be**- (anapest – see 'A Note on Metre')
rack – *stretch*

idea – *thought/image*   Th'i-**de**-a (equiv. 3 syl.)
study of imagination – *reveries*
organ – *approximates aspect/element*
come . . . habit – *appear wearing finer clothes*

prospect – *sightline*

interest in – *a claim on*; liver – *supposedly the organ for passionate feeling*

Will fashion the event in better shape
Than I can lay it down in likelihood.   235
But if all aim but this be levell'd false,
The supposition of the lady's death
Will quench the wonder of her infamy.
And if it sort not well, you may conceal her
As best befits her wounded reputation,   240
In some reclusive and religious life,
Out of all eyes, tongues, minds and injuries.

BENEDICK
Signor Leonato, let the friar advise you,
And though you know my inwardness and love
Is very much unto the prince and Claudio,   245
Yet, by mine honour, I will deal in this
As secretly and justly as your soul
Should with your body.

LEONATO   Being that I flow in grief,
The smallest twine may lead me.

FRIAR
'Tis well consented. Presently away,   250
For to strange sores strangely they strain the cure.
Come, lady, die to live. This wedding day
Perhaps is but prolong'd. Have patience and endure.

Exeunt [all but Beatrice and Benedick].

BENEDICK
Lady Beatrice, have you wept all this while?

BEATRICE
Yea, and I will weep awhile longer.   255

if . . . false – *if all our other goals fail*

quench . . . infamy – *put an end to gossip about her transgression*
if it sort not well – *if things do not turn out well*

conceal . . . injuries – *Hero will be got quietly out of the way if her reputation is not repaired*

inwardness – *close confidence*

flow – *am swept away by (with suggestion of tears)*   Metre – if shared, this line is 12 syl.
    Metre – line is short by 3 syl.

Presently – *Swiftly*   The Friar has 4 lines of AB rhyme.
to . . . cure – *one applies unusual remedies to aid unusual ills*

    Metre – 12 syl. line

The scene moves from VERSE to PROSE.
It is most unusual for a romantic declaration scene like this one to be in prose.

BENEDICK
  I will not desire that.

BEATRICE
  You have no reason; I do it freely.

BENEDICK
  Surely I do believe your fair cousin is
  wronged.

BEATRICE
  Ah, how much might the man deserve of me   260
  that would right her!

BENEDICK
  Is there any way to show such friendship?

BEATRICE
  A very even way, but no such friend.

BENEDICK
  May a man do it?

BEATRICE
  It is a man's office, but not yours.   265

BENEDICK
  I do love nothing in the world so well as you.
  Is not that strange?

BEATRICE
  As strange as the thing I know not. It were as
  possible for me to say I loved nothing so well as you.

even – *direct*

office – *role*; but not yours – *(Benedick has no official alliance with her family, as yet)*

But believe me not – and yet I lie not. I confess nothing,   270
nor I deny nothing. I am sorry for my cousin.

BENEDICK
By my sword, Beatrice, thou lovest me.

BEATRICE
Do not swear and eat it.

BENEDICK
I will swear by it that you love me, and I will
make him eat it that says I love not you.   275

BEATRICE
Will you not eat your word?

BENEDICK
With no sauce that can be devised to it. I
protest I love thee.

BEATRICE
Why then, God forgive me.

BENEDICK
What offence, sweet Beatrice?   280

BEATRICE
You have stayed me in a happy hour; I was
about to protest I loved you.

BENEDICK
And do it, with all thy heart.

By my sword – *(the repository of a gentleman's honour and therefore good for an oath)*

swear and eat it – *play on both to eat one's words and to force someone to eat one's sword*

devised – *invented*

stayed – *stopped*; happy hour – *lucky moment*

BEATRICE

I love you with so much of my heart that none
is left to protest.   285

BENEDICK

Come, bid me do anything for thee.

BEATRICE

Kill Claudio.

BENEDICK

Ha, not for the wide world.

BEATRICE

You kill me to deny it. Farewell. [*Moves as if to
leave.*]

BENEDICK

Tarry, sweet Beatrice. [*Stays her.*]   290

BEATRICE

I am gone, though I am here. There is no love
in you; nay, I pray you, let me go.

BENEDICK

Beatrice –

BEATRICE

In faith, I will go.

BENEDICK

We'll be friends first.   295

deny – *refuse*

I am gone – *(Benedick must be physically preventing Beatrice from leaving here)*

BEATRICE

You dare easier be friends with me than fight
with mine enemy.

BENEDICK

Is Claudio thine enemy?

BEATRICE

Is 'a not approved in the height a villain, that
hath slandered, scorned, dishonoured my kinswoman?   300
O, that I were a man! What, bear her in hand until they
come to take hands, and then with public accusation,
uncovered slander, unmitigated rancour? O God, that I
were a man! I would eat his heart in the marketplace.

BENEDICK

Hear me, Beatrice –   305

BEATRICE

Talk with a man out at a window! A proper
saying!

BENEDICK

Nay, but Beatrice –

BEATRICE

Sweet Hero! She is wronged, she is slandered,
she is undone.   310

BENEDICK

Beat –

BEATRICE

Princes and counties! Surely a princely

'a – *he*; approved in the height – *proven in the highest degree*

bear her in hand – *keep her close (as if all is well)*
take hands – *(in the marriage ceremony)*
uncovered – *bald*

proper – *likely*

undone – *ruined*

counties – *counts*

testimony, a goodly count! Count Comfit, a sweet
gallant surely. O that I were a man for his sake! Or
that I had any friend would be a man for my sake!   315
But manhood is melted into curtsies, valour into
compliment, and men are only turned into tongue,
and trim ones, too. He is now as valiant as Hercules
that only tells a lie and swears it. I cannot be a man
with wishing, therefore I will die a woman with grieving. 320

BENEDICK
Tarry, good Beatrice. By this hand, I love thee.

BEATRICE
Use it for my love some other way than
swearing by it.

BENEDICK
Think you in your soul the Count Claudio
hath wronged Hero?   325

BEATRICE
Yea, as sure as I have a thought or a soul.

BENEDICK
Enough, I am engaged. I will challenge him. I
will kiss your hand, and so I leave you. By this hand,
Claudio shall render me a dear account. As you hear of
me, so think of me. Go comfort your cousin. I must say   330
she is dead, and so farewell.

[Exeunt by different doors.]

Comfit – *sweetmeat/confection/concoction*

curtsies – *fine, affected manners*

trim – *glib/ornamented*
Hercules – (see Myth)

Yea – *Yes* (Pron. yay)

engaged – *contracted*
By this hand – *(can be Beatrice's hand, which he has just kissed, or his own sword hand)*

ACT 4, SCENE 2

Enter the constables[, DOGBERRY and VERGES],
and the [Sexton as] town clerk, in gowns, [with the
Watch,] BORACHIO [and CONRADE].

DOGBERRY
   Is our whole dissembly appeared?

VERGES
   O, a stool and a cushion for the sexton.

SEXTON [*Sits.*]
   Which be the malefactors?

DOGBERRY
   Marry, that am I, and my partner.

VERGES
   Nay, that's certain; we have the exhibition to   5
   examine.

SEXTON
   But which are the offenders that are to be
   examined? [*to Dogberry*] Let them come before, master
   constable.

DOGBERRY
   Yea, marry, let them come before me. [*Watch*   10
   lead Borachio and Conrade forward, then step back.]
   [*to Borachio*] What is your name, friend?

BORACHIO
   Borachio.

SD Q/F *Enter the constables, Borachio and the towne clerke in gownes*

dissembly – *for assembly*   SP Rowe – Dogberry/Verges Q/F – see Intro.

malefactors – *seems to take to mean 'factors', which meant stewards*

exhibition – *for commission*

before – *out in front*   Punct. Arden 3 – before, master Q/F – before master

Yea, marry – *Yes, indeed*

DOGBERRY

[*to the Sexton*] Pray write down 'Borachio'. [*to Conrade*] Yours, sirrah?

CONRADE

I am a gentleman, sir, and my name is   15
Conrade.

DOGBERRY

Write down 'master gentleman Conrade'.
Masters, do you serve God?

CONRADE, BORACHIO

[Yea, sir, we hope.

DOGBERRY

Write down, that they hope they serve God;   20
and write God first, for God defend but God should
go before such villains.] Masters, it is proved already
that you are little better than false knaves, and it will
go near to be thought so shortly. How answer you for
yourselves?   25

CONRADE

Marry, sir, we say we are none.

DOGBERRY

A marvellous witty fellow, I assure you. But I
will go a bout with him. [*to Borachio*] Come you hither,
sirrah. A word in your ear. Sir, I say to you, it is thought
you are false knaves.   30

BORACHIO

Sir, I say to you, we are none.

sirrah – *fellow (not a respectful form of address)*

Yea – *Yes* (Pron. yay)   Q – Yea . . . villains – passage absent in F

God defend but – *God forbid that is should be otherwise*

it will . . . shortly – *it will soon be known*

Marry – *Indeed*

a bout – *a round in fencing*; hither – *here*

DOGBERRY

    Well, stand aside. 'Fore God, they are both
    in a tale. [*to the Sexton*] Have you writ down, that they
    are none?

SEXTON

    Master constable, you go not the way to   35
    examine. You must call forth the watch that are their
    accusers.

DOGBERRY

    Yea, marry, that's the eftest way. Let the
    watch come forth. [*Watch come forward.*] Masters, I
    charge you in the prince's name, accuse these men.   40

1 WATCHMAN

    [*Indicates Borachio.*] This man said, sir,
    that Don John the prince's brother was a villain.

DOGBERRY

    Write down 'Prince John a villain'. Why, this
    is flat perjury, to call a prince's brother villain!

BORACHIO

    Master constable –   45

DOGBERRY

    Pray thee, fellow, peace! I do not like thy look,
    I promise thee.

SEXTON

    What heard you him say else?

2 WATCHMAN

    Marry, that he had received a thousand

'Fore God – *Before God (a way of swearing truth)*
both in a tale – *sharing a lie*

eftest – *invented word aiming to mean most deft or efficacious*

perjury – *(it would actually be slander, but also mistakes the point)*

peace – *silence*

Marry – *Truthfully*

ducats of Don John for accusing the Lady Hero   50
wrongfully.

DOGBERRY
Flat burglary as ever was committed!

VERGES
Yea, by mass, that it is.

SEXTON
What else, fellow?

1 WATCHMAN
And that Count Claudio did mean, upon   55
his words, to disgrace Hero before the whole assembly,
and not marry her.

DOGBERRY
O villain! Thou wilt be condemned into
everlasting redemption for this.

SEXTON
What else?   60

WATCH
This is all.

SEXTON
And this is more, masters, than you can deny.
Prince John is this morning secretly stolen away;
Hero was in this manner accused, in this very manner
refused and, upon the grief of this, suddenly died.   65
Master constable, let these men be bound and brought

burglary – *for perjury*

upon his words – *on the basis of Borachio's words*

redemption – *for perdition*

Prince ... away – *(this is the first news of Don John's flight)*

to Leonato's. I will go before and show him their
examination.   [*Exit.*]

DOGBERRY
Come, let them be opinioned.

VERGES
Let them be in the hands – [*Watch move to bind*   70
them.]

CONRADE
Off, coxcomb!

DOGBERRY
God's my life, where's the sexton? Let him
write down the prince's officer coxcomb! Come, bind
them. [*to Conrade, who resists*] Thou naughty varlet!

CONRADE
Away! You are an ass, you are an ass!   75

DOGBERRY
Dost thou not suspect my place? Dost thou
not suspect my years? O, that he were here to write me
down an ass! But masters, remember that I am an ass;
though it be not written down, yet forget not that I am
an ass. No, thou villain, thou art full of piety, as shall be   80
proved upon thee by good witness. I am a wise fellow,
and which is more, an officer, and which is more, a
householder, and which is more, as pretty a piece of
flesh as any is in Messina, and one that knows the law
– go to! – and a rich fellow enough – go to! – and a   85
fellow that hath had losses, and one that hath two

before – *ahead*

opinioned – *for pinioned (i.e. have their arms bound)*

coxcomb – *an ostentatiously foolish man (from the fool's cap)*

God's my life – *(a common expletive)*

naughty varlet – *wicked rascal*

suspect – *for respect*
he – *i.e. the Sexton, who has already left*

piety – *for impiety*

householder – *owner of property and therefore citizen*
as pretty . . . flesh – *as fine a body*

hath had losses – *can afford to sustain financial setbacks*

gowns, and everything handsome about him. – Bring
him away. – O, that I had been writ down an ass!

Exeunt.

ACT 5, SCENE 1

Enter LEONATO and his brother [ANTONIO].

ANTONIO
    If you go on thus you will kill yourself,
    And 'tis not wisdom thus to second grief
    Against yourself.

LEONATO   I pray thee cease thy counsel,
    Which falls into mine ears as profitless
    As water in a sieve. Give not me counsel,   5
    Nor let no comforter delight mine ear
    But such a one whose wrongs do suit with mine.
    Bring me a father that so lov'd his child,
    Whose joy of her is overwhelm'd like mine,
    And bid him speak of patience.   10
    Measure his woe the length and breadth of mine,
    And let it answer every strain for strain,
    As thus for thus, and such a grief for such,
    In every lineament, branch, shape and form.
    If such a one will smile, and stroke his beard   15
    And sorrow; wag, cry 'hem', when he should groan,
    Patch grief with proverbs, make misfortune drunk
    With candle-wasters, bring him yet to me,
    And I of him will gather patience.
    But there is no such man. For, brother, men   20
    Can counsel and speak comfort to that grief

hath two gowns – *yet still has the means to be well dressed*

This scene is in VERSE until Benedick's entrance.

second . . . yourself – *act as the second to your own adversary (here, grief) in a duel*

Q – comforter F – comfort

suit with – *match*   Q – do F – doth

overwhelm'd – *engulfed*

Metre – this line is short by 2 or 3 syl.

answer every strain – *respond to stress/musical notes*

wag – *jest*; cry 'hem' – *prepare to make speeches (by clearing the throat)*
Patch . . . proverbs – *Mend grief by offering platitudes*
candle-wasters – *those who stay up late*; yet – *then*
I . . . patience – *I will learn my patience from him*   **pat**-i-**ence** (equiv. 3 syl.)

Which they themselves not feel. But tasting it,
Their counsel turns to passion which before
Would give preceptial medicine to rage,
Fetter strong madness in a silken thread,   25
Charm ache with air and agony with words.
No, no, 'tis all men's office to speak patience
To those that wring under the load of sorrow,
But no man's virtue nor sufficiency
To be so moral when he shall endure   30
The like himself. Therefore give me no counsel;
My griefs cry louder than advertisement.

ANTONIO
Therein do men from children nothing differ.

LEONATO
I pray thee peace; I will be flesh and blood.
For there was never yet philosopher   35
That could endure the toothache patiently,
However they have writ the style of gods
And made a push at chance and sufferance.

ANTONIO
Yet bend not all the harm upon yourself;
Make those that do offend you suffer too.   40

LEONATO
There thou speak'st reason. Nay, I will do so:
My soul doth tell me Hero is belied,
And that shall Claudio know, so shall the prince
And all of them that thus dishonour her.

Enter DON PEDRO and CLAUDIO.

give preceptial medicine – *seek to cure with instruction*
Fetter – *Chain*

office – *task*
wring – *writhe*
no . . . sufficiency – *no man is virtuous enough*
To be . . . himself – *To adhere to this moral when experiencing the same thing*

advertisement – *advisement (with a pun on crying news in the streets)*

philosopher – *(here with the stoics in mind)*

writ . . . gods – *wise men who have written as if above human behaviour*
made . . . sufferance – *scoffed at reacting to misfortune and suffering*

ANTONIO
Here comes the prince and Claudio hastily.   45

DON PEDRO
Good e'en, good e'en.

CLAUDIO   Good day to both of you.

LEONATO
Hear you, my lords?

DON PEDRO   We have some haste, Leonato.

LEONATO
Some haste, my lord! Well, fare you well, my lord.
Are you so hasty now? Well, all is one.

DON PEDRO
Nay, do not quarrel with us, good old man.   50

ANTONIO
If he could right himself with quarrelling,
Some of us would lie low.

CLAUDIO   Who wrongs him?

LEONATO
Marry, thou dost wrong me, thou dissembler, thou!
Nay, never lay thy hand upon thy sword;
I fear thee not.

CLAUDIO   Marry, beshrew my hand   55
If it should give your age such cause of fear.
In faith, my hand meant nothing to my sword.

hastily – *(a useful SD)*

e'en – *evening*

all is one – *it's all the same to me*

lie low – *be cut down*

Metre – shared line is short by 1 syl.

Marry – *Indeed*; dissembler – *liar*   Ma-rry, **thou** (anapest – see 'A Note on Metre')

Marry – *Truthfully*; beshrew – *curse*

In . . . sword – *I had no intention of drawing my sword*

LEONATO

Tush, tush, man, never fleer and jest at me!
I speak not like a dotard nor a fool,
As under privilege of age to brag   60
What I have done being young, or what would do
Were I not old. Know, Claudio, to thy head,
Thou hast so wrong'd mine innocent child and me
That I am forced to lay my reverence by,
And with grey hairs and bruise of many days   65
Do challenge thee to trial of a man.
I say thou hast belied mine innocent child.
Thy slander hath gone through and through her heart,
And she lies buri'd with her ancestors –
O, in a tomb where never scandal slept,   70
Save this of hers, framed by thy villainy.

CLAUDIO

My villainy?

LEONATO   Thine, Claudio; thine, I say.

DON PEDRO

You say not right, old man.

LEONATO   My lord, my lord,
I'll prove it on his body, if he dare,
Despite his nice fence and his active practice,   75
His May of youth and bloom of lustihood.

CLAUDIO

Away! I will not have to do with you.

Tush – *(dismissive expletive)*; fleer – *jeer*
dotard – *someone who has lost their wits with age*
As . . . brag – *i.e. he is not hiding behind his elderly status*   **priv**-il-**ege** (equiv. 3 syl.)

being (equiv. 1 syl.)

to thy head – *I say this to your face*

inn-ocent (equiv. 2 syl); F – mine Q – my
reverence – *dignity earned by age*   **rev**-erance (equiv. 2 syl.)

trial of a man – *a duel*   **tri**-al (equiv. 2 syl.)

inn-ocent (equiv. 2 syl.)

framed – *constructed*

nice . . . practice – *his currently practised skill in swordsmanship*
lustihood – *vigour*

LEONATO

    Canst thou so doff me? Thou hast kill'd my child;
    If thou kill'st me, boy, thou shalt kill a man.

ANTONIO

    He shall kill two of us, and men indeed.   80
    But that's no matter, let him kill one first.
    Win me and wear me! Let him answer me.
    Come, follow me, boy. Come, sir boy, come, follow me,
    Sir boy! I'll whip you from your foining fence!
    Nay, as I am a gentleman, I will.   85

LEONATO

    Brother –

ANTONIO

    Content yourself. God knows, I loved my niece,
    And she is dead, slander'd to death by villains
    That dare as well answer a man indeed
    As I dare take a serpent by the tongue.   90
    Boys, apes, braggarts, jacks, milksops!

LEONATO   Brother Anthony –

ANTONIO

    Hold you content. What, man? I know them, yea,
    And what they weigh, even to the utmost scruple.
    Scambling, outfacing, fashion-monging boys,
    That lie, and cog, and flout, deprave and slander,   95
    Go anticly and show outward hideousness,
    And speak off half a dozen dangerous words
    How they might hurt their enemies, if they durst –
    And this is all.

doff – *put off*

Win me and wear me – *Defeat me and flaunt your win*

Metre – 12 syl. line

foining fence – *thrusting with a foil (sees modern duelling as inferior to old fashioned slashing)*

Metre – this line is short by 8 syl. or may be considered extra-metrical

Content yourself – *Patience* (do not interrupt me)

braggarts – *empty boasters*; jacks – *knaves*; milksops – *weaklings*

Metre – if shared, this line is 12 syl.

Hold you content – *Stay patient*

what . . . scruple – *what their value is, to the smallest increment*   even (equiv. 1 syl.)

Scambling – *Confrontational*; outfacing – *brazen*; fashion-monging – *foppish*

cog – *cheat*; flout – *mock*

Go . . . hideousness – *behave like fools, while appearing fierce*   – tic-ly **and** (anapest)

dan-gerous (equiv. 2 syl.)

durst – *dared*   **en**-emies (equiv. 2 syl.)

Ambiguous metrical connection – see Series Introduction

LEONATO   But brother Anthony –

ANTONIO   Come, 'tis no matter.
Do not you meddle; let me deal in this.   100

DON PEDRO
Gentlemen both, we will not wake your patience.
My heart is sorry for your daughter's death,
But on my honour she was charg'd with nothing
But what was true and very full of proof.

LEONATO
My lord, my lord –

DON PEDRO   I will not hear you.

LEONATO   No?   105
– Come, brother, away. I will be heard.

ANTONIO
And shall, or some of us will smart for it.

Exeunt Leonato and Antonio.

Enter BENEDICK.

DON PEDRO
See, see: here comes the man we went to seek.

CLAUDIO
Now, signor, what news?

BENEDICK
[*to Don Pedro*] Good day, my lord.   110

wake your patience – *require your forbearance*

hear you – *entertain your grievance*

An ambiguous metrical connection (in Q and F 'No' is lineated with the rest of
be heard – *have my challenge answered*   Leonato's line)

smart – *feel pain*

The scene moves from VERSE to PROSE.

DON PEDRO

Welcome, signor. You are almost come to
part almost a fray.

CLAUDIO

We had liked to have had our two noses
snapped off with two old men without teeth.

DON PEDRO

Leonato and his brother. What think'st   115
thou? Had we fought, I doubt we should have been too
young for them.

BENEDICK

In a false quarrel there is no true valour. I
came to seek you both.

CLAUDIO

We have been up and down to seek thee, for   120
we are high-proof melancholy and would fain have it
beaten away. Wilt thou use thy wit?

BENEDICK

It is in my scabbard. Shall I draw it?

DON PEDRO

Dost thou wear thy wit by thy side?

CLAUDIO

Never any did so, though very many have   125
been beside their wit. I will bid thee draw as we do the
minstrels – draw to pleasure us.

part almost a fray – *break up a fight.*

high-proof melancholy – *in the highest proportion of sadness;* fain – *wish*

scabbard – *sword sheath*

wit by thy side – *beside himself/out of his wits*

draw . . . minstrels – *as a musician draws music from the instrument*

DON PEDRO

As I am an honest man, he looks pale. Art
thou sick, or angry?

CLAUDIO

What, courage, man! What though care killed a   130
cat, thou hast mettle enough in thee to kill care.

BENEDICK

Sir, I shall meet your wit in the career an you
charge it against me. I pray you choose another subject.

CLAUDIO

Nay, then, give him another staff; this last was
broke cross.   135

DON PEDRO

By this light, he changes more and more. I
think he be angry indeed.

CLAUDIO

If he be, he knows how to turn his girdle.

BENEDICK

Shall I speak a word in your ear?

CLAUDIO

God bless me from a challenge.   140

BENEDICK

[*aside to Claudio*] You are a villain. I jest not.
I will make it good how you dare, with what you dare
and when you dare. Do me right, or I will protest

Art . . . angry – *Benedick earlier stated he would look pale with anger or sickness, but not love*

care killed a cat – *Prov.: of little meaning*
mettle – *spirit*

career – *full gallop*; an – *if*
charge – *(as in jousting or battle)*

staff – *lance*
broke cross – *(sign of an inept jousting attempt)*

turn his girdle – *Prov.: unclear if this means prepare to fight, or indicate refusal to fight*

God . . . challenge – *Surely this cannot be a challenge*

make it good – *duel (as Benedick is the challenger he offers Claudio choice of conditions)*

your cowardice. You have killed a sweet lady, and
her death shall fall heavy on you. Let me hear from   145
you.

CLAUDIO
Well, I will meet you, so I may have good cheer.

DON PEDRO
What, a feast, a feast?

CLAUDIO
I'faith, I thank him, he hath bid me to a calf's
head and a capon, the which if I do not carve most   150
curiously, say my knife's naught. Shall I not find a
woodcock too?

BENEDICK
Sir, your wit ambles well; it goes easily.

DON PEDRO
I'll tell thee how Beatrice praised thy wit the
other day. I said thou hadst a fine wit. 'True,' said she,   155
'a fine little one.' 'No,' said I, 'a great wit.' 'Right,' says
she, 'a great gross one.' 'Nay,' said I, 'a good wit.' 'Just,'
said she, 'it hurts nobody.' 'Nay,' said I, 'the gentleman
is wise.' 'Certain,' said she, 'a wise gentleman.' 'Nay,'
said I, 'he hath the tongues.' 'That I believe,' said she,   160
'for he swore a thing to me on Monday night, which
he forswore on Tuesday morning. There's a double
tongue; there's two tongues.' Thus did she an hour
together trans-shape thy particular virtues. Yet at last
she concluded, with a sigh, thou wast the properest   165
man in Italy.

good cheer – *a good enough competition*

a feast – *(Don Pedro suggests good cheer in the more common manner)*

bid – *invited*; calf's . . . capon – *feast foods doubling as insults*; calf – *fool*
capon – *coward (literally a castrated cockerel)*
carve . . . curiously – *if he doesn't cut Benedick up skilfully*; naught – *nothing*
woodcock – *supposed to be a foolish bird*

ambles – *walks at an easy pace*

fine – *Beatrice (allegedly) plays on its meaning of delicate*   Q – said she F – says she

a wise gentleman – *(common joke when meaning a fool)*
hath the tongues – *speaks several languages*

an hour together – *for a full hour*
trans-shape – *transform*
properest – *most admirable*

CLAUDIO

For the which she wept heartily and said she
cared not.

DON PEDRO

Yea, that she did, but yet for all that, an if she
did not hate him deadly, she would love him dearly.   170
The old man's daughter told us all.

CLAUDIO

All, all. And moreover, God saw him when he
was hid in the garden.

DON PEDRO

But when shall we set the savage bull's horns
on the sensible Benedick's head?   175

CLAUDIO

Yea, and text underneath: 'Here dwells Benedick
the married man.'

BENEDICK

Fare you well. Boy, you know my mind. I will
leave you now to your gossip-like humour. You break
jests as braggarts do their blades, which, God be   180
thanked, hurt not. My lord, for your many courtesies,
I thank you. I must discontinue your company. Your
brother the bastard is fled from Messina; you have
among you killed a sweet and innocent lady. For my
Lord Lack-beard there, he and I shall meet, and till   185
then peace be with him.   [*Exit.*]

DON PEDRO

He is in earnest.

daughter – *i.e. Hero*

God . . . garden – *ref. Adam hiding his nakedness* (Bib.)/*Benedick hiding to hear his friends talk*

braggarts . . . blades – *coward soldiers break their own swords, pretending to have been in a fight*
discontinue your company – *a formal resignation from Don Pedro's company at arms*

Lack-beard – *(with 'boy', Benedick emphasizes Claudio's lack of full manhood)*; meet – *duel*

CLAUDIO

In most profound earnest. And, I'll warrant
you, for the love of Beatrice.

DON PEDRO

And hath challenged thee?   190

CLAUDIO

Most sincerely.

DON PEDRO

What a pretty thing man is when he goes in
his doublet and hose, and leaves off his wit!

CLAUDIO

He is then a giant to an ape; but then is an ape
a doctor to such a man.   195

DON PEDRO

But soft you, let me be. Pluck up, my heart,
and be sad – did he not say my brother was fled?

*Enter Constables [DOGBERRY and VERGES, with the
Watch], CONRADE and BORACHIO.*

DOGBERRY

Come you, sir. If justice cannot tame you, she
shall ne'er weigh more reasons in her balance. Nay, an
you be a cursing hypocrite once, you must be looked to.   200

DON PEDRO

How now? Two of my brother's men bound?
Borachio one.

warrant – *wager*

pretty – *fine*
doublet and hose – *standard jacket and leggings combination for men*

He . . . man – *a fool thinks such a man very grand, but the fool is in fact a scholar by comparison*

soft you – *wait a moment*; Pluck up – *Pull yourself together*
sad – *serious*

If . . . balance – *If justice cannot deal with you, she might as well give up her job*
reasons – *arguments*; balance – *scales*

bound – *an indication that they should be visibly restrained*

CLAUDIO
Hearken after their offence, my lord.

DON PEDRO
Officers, what offence have these men done?

DOGBERRY
Marry, sir, they have committed false report.   205
Moreover they have spoken untruths, secondarily they
are slanders, sixth and lastly, they have belied a lady,
thirdly they have verified unjust things, and, to
conclude, they are lying knaves.

DON PEDRO
First I ask thee what they have done, thirdly   210
I ask thee what's their offence, sixth and lastly why they
are committed, and, to conclude, what you lay to their
charge?

CLAUDIO
Rightly reasoned and in his own division; and,
by my troth, there's one meaning well suited.   215

DON PEDRO
Who have you offended, masters, that you
are thus bound to your answer? This learned constable
is too cunning to be understood. What's your offence?

BORACHIO
Sweet Prince, let me go no farther to mine
answer. Do you hear me, and let this count kill me. I   220
have deceived even your very eyes. What your wisdoms
could not discover, these shallow fools have brought to
light, who in the night overheard me confessing to this

Hearken after – *Enquire after*

Marry – *Indeed*
Moreover . . . conclude – *(Dogberry is attempting to imitate the form of a logical proposition)*

Rightly . . . division – *Well laid out according to his method.*
by my troth – *truthfully*; one . . . suited – *a well-appointed answer*

bound to your answer – *compelled to answer and to adhere to it*
cunning – *ingenious*

let me . . . answer – *let me not prevaricate*

man how Don John your brother incensed me to
slander the lady Hero; how you were brought into   225
the orchard and saw me court Margaret in Hero's
garments; how you disgraced her when you should
marry her. My villainy they have upon record, which I
had rather seal with my death than repeat over to my
shame. The lady is dead upon mine and my master's   230
false accusation, and, briefly, I desire nothing but the
reward of a villain.

DON PEDRO
Runs not this speech like iron through your blood?

CLAUDIO
I have drunk poison whiles he utter'd it.

DON PEDRO
But did my brother set thee on to this?   235

BORACHIO
Yea, and paid me richly for the practice of it.

DON PEDRO
He is compos'd and fram'd of treachery,
And fled he is upon this villainy.

CLAUDIO
Sweet Hero! Now thy image doth appear
In the rare semblance that I loved it first.   240

DOGBERRY
Come, bring away the plaintiffs. By this
time our sexton hath reformed Signor Leonato of the

incensed – *incited*

repeat over – *recount*

iron – *cold and dead*   Lines 235–42 are in VERSE; **i**-ron (equiv. 2 syl.)

Yea, and **paid** (anapest – see 'A Note on Metre')

fram'd – *built*

rare semblance – *fine appearance*

DOGBERRY and VERGES speak in PROSE.

reformed – *for informed*

matter. And masters, do not forget to specify, when
time and place shall serve, that I am an ass.

VERGES

Here, here comes master Signor Leonato, and   245
the sexton too.

Enter LEONATO, his brother [ANTONIO] and the Sexton.

LEONATO

Which is the villain? Let me see his eyes,
That when I note another man like him
I may avoid him. Which of these is he?

BORACHIO

If you would know your wronger, look on me.   250

LEONATO

Art thou the slave that with thy breath hast kill'd
Mine innocent child?

BORACHIO   Yea, even I alone.

LEONATO

No, not so, villain, thou beliest thyself.
Here stand a pair of honourable men;
A third is fled that had a hand in it.   255
I thank you, princes, for my daughter's death;
Record it with your high and worthy deeds.
'Twas bravely done, if you bethink you of it.

CLAUDIO

I know not how to pray your patience.
Yet I must speak. Choose your revenge yourself.   260

The scene moves back into VERSE.

-no-cent **child** (anapest see 'A Note on Metre')

beliest thyself – *tells lies against himself*   Q – thou F – thou thou
honourable men – *Don Pedro and Claudio*

pat-i-**ence** (3 syl.)

Impose me to what penance your invention
Can lay upon my sin. Yet sinn'd I not
But in mistaking.

DON PEDRO   By my soul, nor I.
And yet to satisfy this good old man
I would bend under any heavy weight   265
That he'll enjoin me to.

LEONATO
I cannot bid you bid my daughter live –
That were impossible. But I pray you both,
Possess the people in Messina here
How innocent she died. [*to Claudio*] And if your love   270
Can labour aught in sad invention,
Hang her an epitaph upon her tomb
And sing it to her bones. Sing it tonight.
Tomorrow morning come you to my house,
And since you could not be my son-in-law,   275
Be yet my nephew. My brother hath a daughter,
Almost the copy of my child that's dead,
And she alone is heir to both of us.
Give her the right you should have given her cousin,
And so dies my revenge.

CLAUDIO   O noble sir!   280
Your over-kindness doth wring tears from me.
I do embrace your offer, and dispose
For henceforth of poor Claudio.

LEONATO
Tomorrow, then, I will expect your coming;
Tonight I take my leave. This naughty man   285

enjoin – *impose*   Metre – this line is short by 4 syl.

pray – *ask*   -si-ble. **But** (anapest – see 'A Note on Metre')
Possess – *Inform*

Can . . . invention – *create any work from imagination*   in-**ven**-ti-**on** (equiv. 4 syl.)

-phew my **bro**- (anapest – see 'A Note on Metre')

given (equiv. 1 syl.)
Claudio's quick response on this split line will suggest sincerity.

Metre – line is short by 2 or 3 syl.

naughty – *wicked*

Shall face to face be brought to Margaret,
Who I believe was pack'd in all this wrong,
Hired to it by your brother.

BORACHIO   No, by my soul she was not,
Nor knew not what she did when she spoke to me,
But always hath been just and virtuous   290
In anything that I do know by her.

DOGBERRY
Moreover, sir, which indeed is not under
white and black, this plaintiff here, the offender, did
call me ass. I beseech you let it be remembered in his
punishment. And also the watch heard them talk of one   295
Deformed; they say he wears a key in his ear and a lock
hanging by it, and borrows money in God's name, the
which he hath used so long, and never paid, that
now men grow hard-hearted and will lend nothing for
God's sake. Pray you examine him upon that point.   300

LEONATO
I thank thee for thy care and honest pains.

DOGBERRY
Your worship speaks like a most thankful and
reverent youth, and I praise God for you.

LEONATO
[*Gives him money.*] There's for thy pains.

DOGBERRY
God save the foundation!   305

pack'd – *incorporated*

Hired (equiv. 1 syl.)

Metre – 14 syl. shared line (Borachio's line may overlap with the previous line) when she **spoke** (anapest – see 'A Note on Metre')

DOGBERRY speaks in PROSE.

under . . . black – *written on the page*

one Deformed – *ref. again to the imagined co-conspirator, 'Deformed'*

Pray . . . point – *Please ask him about that*

LEONATO's line is in VERSE.

reverent – *reverend*; youth – *for elder*

pains – *trouble*

God . . . foundation – *standard response to being given charitable alms*

LEONATO

Go, I discharge thee of thy prisoner, and I
thank thee.

DOGBERRY

I leave an arrant knave with your worship,
which I beseech your worship to correct yourself, for
the example of others. God keep your worship! I wish   310
your worship well! God restore you to health! I humbly
give you leave to depart, and if a merry meeting may be
wished, God prohibit it! Come, neighbour.

[Exeunt Dogberry and Verges.]

LEONATO

Until tomorrow morning, lords, farewell.

ANTONIO

Farewell, my lords. We look for you tomorrow.   315

DON PEDRO

We will not fail.

CLAUDIO   Tonight I'll mourn with Hero.

LEONATO *[to the Watch]*

Bring you these fellows on. We'll talk with Margaret,
How her acquaintance grew with this lewd fellow.

Exeunt.

correct – *punish*

give – *for ask*
prohibit – *for permit*

The scene moves back into VERSE.

look for you – *expect you*

Mar-gret – equiv. 2 syl. with fem. ending

lewd – *low*

ACT 5, SCENE 2

Enter BENEDICK *and* MARGARET.

BENEDICK
Pray thee, sweet mistress Margaret, deserve
well at my hands by helping me to the speech of
Beatrice.

MARGARET
Will you then write me a sonnet in praise of
my beauty?   5

BENEDICK
In so high a style, Margaret, that no man
living shall come over it; for in most comely truth thou
deservest it.

MARGARET
To have no man come over me? Why, shall I
always keep below stairs?   10

BENEDICK
Thy wit is as quick as the greyhound's mouth,
it catches.

MARGARET
And yours as blunt as the fencer's foils, which
hit, but hurt not.

BENEDICK
A most manly wit, Margaret, it will not hurt a   15
woman. And so, I pray thee, call Beatrice. I give thee
the bucklers.

high a style – *(the style favoured by noblemen writing love poetry)*
come over it – *reach higher/top it*; comely – *fair*

To . . . me? – *never be seduced/never bed a man of higher status*
keep below stairs – *be subservient*

foils – *swords with blunted tips*

give thee the bucklers – *grant you victory (in the battle of wits)*

MARGARET

Give us the swords; we have bucklers of our
own.

BENEDICK

If you use them, Margaret, you must put in   20
the pikes with a vice, and they are dangerous weapons
for maids.

MARGARET

Well, I will call Beatrice to you, who I think
hath legs.   *Exit.*

BENEDICK

And therefore will come.   25
[*Sings.*]
    The God of love
    That sits above,
    And knows me, and knows me,
    How pitiful I deserve –
I mean in singing; but in loving, Leander the good   30
swimmer, Troilus the first employer of pandars and
a whole bookful of these quondam carpet-mongers,
whose names yet run smoothly in the even road of a
blank verse, why, they were never so truly turned over
and over as my poor self in love. Marry, I cannot show   35
it in rhyme. I have tried; I can find out no rhyme to
'lady' but 'baby' – an innocent rhyme; for 'scorn', 'horn'
– a hard rhyme; for 'school', 'fool', a babbling rhyme:
very ominous endings. No, I was not born under a
rhyming planet nor I cannot woo in festival terms.   40

Enter BEATRICE.

swords – *penises*; bucklers – *small, round, shields/women's bellies or genitals*

them – *i.e. bucklers*; put . . . vice – *fix the spike in the middle of the shield with a screw* dangerous . . . maids – *virgins' vaginas encountering penises will get into trouble* Margaret and Benedick are having possibly the filthiest conversation in the play.

The God . . . deserve – *(a popular ballad, not a work of his own invention)*

How pitiful – *How much pity* I mean in singing – *(the quality of his singing should inspire pity)*; Leander – (see Myth) pandars – *procurers*; Leander and Troilus were both tragic lovers, so poor role models quondam – *former*, carpet-mongers – *knights rewarded for courtly rather than battle feats* yet – *still* verse – *lovers were expected to be great writers of poetry* Marry – *Truthfully*

innocent – *childish/silly* 'baby' . . . 'horn' . . . 'fool' – *(his sequence of word matches invokes the fate of a cuckold)* ominous endings – *portents of doom/poor rhymes* rhyming planet – *astrological sign that gives poetic skill*; Q – nor F – for festival – *joyful*

Sweet Beatrice, wouldst thou come when I called thee?

BEATRICE

Yea, signor, and depart when you bid me.

BENEDICK

O, stay but till then.

BEATRICE

'Then' is spoken; fare you well now. And yet,
ere I go, let me go with that I came for, which is, with   45
knowing what hath passed between you and Claudio.

BENEDICK

Only foul words – and thereupon I will kiss
thee.

BEATRICE

Foul words is but foul wind, and foul wind is
but foul breath, and foul breath is noisome, therefore I   50
will depart unkissed.

BENEDICK

Thou hast frighted the word out of his right
sense, so forcible is thy wit. But I must tell thee plainly:
Claudio undergoes my challenge, and either I must
shortly hear from him, or I will subscribe him a coward.   55
And I pray thee now tell me, for which of my bad parts
didst thou first fall in love with me?

BEATRICE

For them all together, which maintained so
politic a state of evil that they will not admit any good

ere – *before*

noisome – *noxious*

undergoes – *is subject to*
subscribe – *proclaim*
bad parts – *(courtly lovers conventionally praised the beloved's discrete parts)*

politic – *well-governed*

part to intermingle with them. But for which of my   60
good parts did you first suffer love for me?

BENEDICK

'Suffer love'! A good epithet. I do suffer love
indeed, for I love thee against my will.

BEATRICE

In spite of your heart, I think. Alas, poor heart!
If you spite it for my sake, I will spite it for yours, for   65
will never love that which my friend hates.

BENEDICK

Thou and I are too wise to woo peaceably.

BEATRICE

It appears not in this confession: there's not
one wise man among twenty that will praise himself.

BENEDICK

An old, an old instance, Beatrice, that lived in   70
the time of good neighbours. If a man do not erect in
this age his own tomb ere he dies, he shall live no longer
in monument than the bell rings and the widow weeps.

BEATRICE

And how long is that, think you?

BENEDICK

Question: why, an hour in clamour and a   75
quarter in rheum. Therefore is it most expedient for
the wise, if Don Worm – his conscience – find no
impediment to the contrary, to be the trumpet of his
own virtues, as I am to myself. So much for praising

suffer – *experience, but with connotations of endure*

good epithet – *choice of word that nails the important thing*

spite – *spurn*

wise – *clever* (but can be taken as its more conventional meaning, too)

It appears . . . himself – *his statement does not show wisdom, as the wise don't praise themselves*

instance – *precept*
lived . . . neighbours – *it applied in the old days when neighbours would still praise one another*
monument – *memory*

hour in clamour – *the tolling of the funeral bell*
quarter – *three months*; rheum – *tears*
Don Worm – *(conscience was portrayed as a worm in Bib. Mark 9.44)*

myself, who I myself will bear witness is praiseworthy.   80
And now tell me, how doth your cousin?

BEATRICE
Very ill.

BENEDICK
And how do you?

BEATRICE
Very ill too.

BENEDICK
Serve God, love me and mend. There will I   85
leave you too, for here comes one in haste.

Enter URSULA.

URSULA
Madam, you must come to your uncle. Yonder's
old coil at home. It is proved my lady Hero hath
been falsely accused, the prince and Claudio mightily
abused, and Don John is the author of all, who is fled   90
and gone. Will you come presently?

BEATRICE
Will you go hear this news, signor?

BENEDICK
I will live in thy heart, die in thy lap, and be
buried in thy eyes – and moreover, I will go with thee
to thy uncle's.   95

Exeunt.

mend – *this will mend the situation*

old coil – *a grand uproar*

abused – *wronged*
presently – *immediately*

die in thy lap – *pledging himself to her for life/sexually climaxing with her*

ACT 5, SCENE 3

> *Enter* CLAUDIO, DON PEDRO, *and three or four*
> *[Attendants, including a Lord and Musicians,] with tapers.*

CLAUDIO
Is this the monument of Leonato?

LORD
It is, my lord. [*Reads the epitaph*]
Done to death by slanderous tongues
Was the Hero that here lies;
Death, in guerdon of her wrongs,   5
Gives her fame which never dies;
So the life that died with shame,
Lives in death with glorious fame.
[*Hangs scroll.*]
Hang thou there upon the tomb,
Praising her when I am dumb.   10

CLAUDIO
Now music sound, and sing your solemn hymn.   [*Music*]

ONE OR MORE SINGERS [*Sing.*]
Pardon, goddess of the night,
Those that slew thy virgin knight,
For the which with songs of woe
Round about her tomb they go.   15
Midnight, assist our moan,
Help us to sigh and groan,
Heavily, heavily.
Graves yawn and yield your dead,
Till death be utterèd,   20
Heavily, heavily.

monument – *family tomb*   The majority of this short scene is in RHYMED
VERSE.

Claudio is presumably the author of the epitaph.   Metre – line is short by 6 syl.
Metre – catalectic trochaic tetrameters (see Intro.)

guerdon – *payment*; wrongs – *the wrongs done against her*

dumb – *silent*

Metre – this song is also in catalectic trochaic tetrameters

goddess of the night – *Artemis/Diana* (see Myth)
virgin knight – *(Hero is being acknowledged as a disciple of Diana, the chaste)*

Metre – 2 pairs of lines of iambic trimeter, broken up with a dactylic refrain,
'heavily'

Graves . . . dead – *no convincing explanation has been proposed for this gothic turn*
utterèd – *spoken*

LORD

    Now unto thy bones good night;
    Yearly will I do this rite.

DON PEDRO

    Good morrow, masters. Put your torches out.
    The wolves have prey'd, and look, the gentle day,   25
    Before the wheels of Phoebus, round about
    Dapples the drowsy east with spots of grey.
    Thanks to you all, and leave us. Fare you well.

CLAUDIO

    Good morrow, masters; each his several way.

DON PEDRO

    Come, let us hence and put on other weeds,   30
    And then to Leonato's we will go.

CLAUDIO

    And Hymen now with luckier issue speed's
    Than this for whom we render'd up this woe.

Exeunt.

ACT 5, SCENE 4

Enter LEONATO, BENEDICK, MARGARET,
URSULA, ANTONIO, FRIAR [Francis],
HERO [and BEATRICE].

FRIAR

    Did I not tell you she was innocent?

SP Lord – a line we might expect to be Claudio's
Metre – these two lines are in catalectic trochaic tetrameter

morrow – *morning*　　　　Don Pedro and Claudio share a passage of AB rhyme

Phoebus (Pron. **Fee**-bus) – *Apollo* (see Myth)

several – *various*

weeds – *garments* (they are in mourning clothes and must change for the wedding)

Hymen – (see Myth); issue – *offspring*; speed's – *send us*　　　**luck**-ier (equiv. 2 syl.)
this – *i.e. Hero*

This scene begins in VERSE.

LEONATO

So are the prince and Claudio who accus'd her,
Upon the error that you heard debated.
But Margaret was in some fault for this,
Although against her will, as it appears   5
In the true course of all the question.

ANTONIO

Well, I am glad that all things sorts so well.

BENEDICK

And so am I, being else by faith enforc'd
To call young Claudio to a reckoning for it.

LEONATO

Well, daughter, and you gentlewomen all,   10
Withdraw into a chamber by yourselves,
And when I send for you, come hither mask'd.
The prince and Claudio promis'd by this hour
To visit me. You know your office, brother:
You must be father to your brother's daughter   15
And give her to young Claudio.

Exeunt Ladies.

ANTONIO

Which I will do with confirm'd countenance.

BENEDICK

Friar, I must entreat your pains, I think.

FRIAR

To do what, signor?

Clau-dio – equiv. 2 syl. throughout this scene

Mar-gar-**et** (equiv. 3 syl.)

against her will – *without intent*

In . . . question – *As it has transpired through our questioning*   **quest**-i-**on** (equiv. 3 syl.)

being . . . enforc'd – *otherwise forced by my honour*   being (equiv. 1 syl.)

reckoning – *account*   **reck**-oning (equiv. 2 syl.)

hither – *out here*

office – *task, role*

be – *act as*   Metre – line is short by 2 or 3 syl.

confirm'd countenance – *serious face/bearing*

entreat your pains – *ask for your assistance*   **Fri**-ar (equiv. 2 syl.)

Metre – line is short by 5 syl.

BENEDICK

To bind me, or undo me, one of them.   20
Signor Leonato – truth it is, good signor,
Your niece regards me with an eye of favour.

LEONATO

That eye my daughter lent her? 'Tis most true.

BENEDICK

And I do with an eye of love requite her.

LEONATO

The sight whereof I think you had from me,   25
From Claudio and the prince. But what's your will?

BENEDICK

Your answer, sir, is enigmatical.
But for my will, my will is your good will
May stand with ours this day to be conjoin'd
In the estate of honourable marriage;   30
In which, good Friar, I shall desire your help.

LEONATO

My heart is with your liking.

FRIAR   And my help.
Here comes the prince and Claudio.

Enter DON PEDRO and CLAUDIO, with Attendants.

DON PEDRO

Good morrow to this fair assembly.

LEONATO

Good morrow, Prince, good morrow, Claudio.   35

bind – *in marriage*; undo – *ruin*

That eye … her – *(referring to Hero's deception of Beatrice)*

hon-our-**ab**-le (equiv. 4 syl.); **mar**-riage (equiv. 2 syl.)

My … liking – *I approve of your desires*   Metre – line is short by 2 or 3 syl.

Clau-di-**o** – reverts to 3 syl. here

We here attend you. Are you yet determin'd
Today to marry with my brother's daughter?

CLAUDIO
I'll hold my mind were she an Ethiope.

LEONATO
Call her forth, brother. Here's the friar ready. [*Exit Antonio.*]

DON PEDRO
Good morrow, Benedick. Why, what's the matter   40
That you have such a February face,
So full of frost, of storm and cloudiness?

CLAUDIO
I think he thinks upon the savage bull.
Tush, fear not, man: we'll tip thy horns with gold,
And all Europa shall rejoice at thee,   45
As once Europa did at lusty Jove
When he would play the noble beast in love.

BENEDICK
Bull Jove, sir, had an amiable low,
And some such strange bull leap'd your father's cow
And got a calf in that same noble feat   50
Much like to you, for you have just his bleat.

*Enter ANTONIO, HERO, BEATRICE, MARGARET
[and] URSULA[, the women masked].*

CLAUDIO
For this I owe you. Here comes other reckonings.
Which is the lady I must seize upon?
[*Antonio leads Hero forward.*]

Are . . . determin'd – *Have you maintained your decision*

Ethiope – *Ethiopian (i.e. were she so far from being fair)*

fri-ar (equiv. 2 syl.)

Why . . . face – *Don Pedro and Claudio seem to have entirely forgotten that Hero is still dead*
February (equiv. 4 syl. – **Feb**-ru-**ar**-y) – *wintery and therefore grim*

Tush – *(dismissive expletive)*; tip thy horns with gold – *make him a glorious cuckold*
Europa – *Europe, the continent, named after* . . .   Source: Ovid, *Metamorphoses*
Europa – *girl whom Jove kidnapped while in the form of a bull* (see Myth)

amiable low – *pleasing moo*   Benedick makes his jest in 2 rhyming couplets.

got – *begat*
strange . . . bleat – *calling Claudio a bastard, as well as a callow fool*

All the women must be veiled or masked so that after Hero is revealed, Beatrice can be too.

reckonings – *accounts/payments*   Metre – 12 syl. line

LEONATO
This same is she, and I do give you her.

CLAUDIO
Why then she's mine. [*to Hero*] Sweet, let me see your face. 55

LEONATO
No, that you shall not till you take her hand
Before this friar and swear to marry her.

CLAUDIO
Give me your hand before this holy friar.
I am your husband, if you like of me.

HERO [*Unmasks.*]
And when I liv'd I was your other wife;   60
And when you lov'd, you were my other husband.

CLAUDIO
Another Hero!

HERO   Nothing certainer.
One Hero died defil'd, but I do live,
And surely as I live, I am a maid.

DON PEDRO
The former Hero! Hero that is dead!   65

LEONATO
She died, my lord, but whiles her slander liv'd.

FRIAR
All this amazement can I qualify,

friar (equiv. 1 syl.)

defil'd – *sullied/slandered*
maid – *virgin*

qualify – *explain*

When after that the holy rites are ended,
I'll tell you largely of fair Hero's death.
Meantime, let wonder seem familiar,   70
And to the chapel let us presently.

BENEDICK
Soft and fair, Friar. Which is Beatrice?

BEATRICE [*Unmasks.*]
I answer to that name. What is your will?

BENEDICK
Do not you love me?

BEATRICE   Why no, no more than reason.

BENEDICK
Why then your uncle and the prince and Claudio   75
Have been deceived – they swore you did.

BEATRICE
Do not you love me?

BENEDICK   Troth no, no more than reason.

BEATRICE
Why then my cousin, Margaret and Ursula
Are much deceiv'd, for they did swear you did.

BENEDICK
They swore that you were almost sick for me.   80

BEATRICE
They swore that you were well-nigh dead for me.

largely – *in detail*
let wonder seem familiar – *behave as if everything is normal* fa-**mil**-i-**ar** – 4 syl.
presently – *immediately*

Soft and fair – *Pause a moment (suggests stage activity as if to exit around him)*

me? Why **no** – (anapest – see 'A Note on Metre')

This line is short by 2 syl. (or 1 if pronounced 'deceivèd')

Troth – *In truth*   me? Troth **no** (anapest – see 'A Note on Metre')

Metre – 12 syl. line

well-nigh – *very nearly*

BENEDICK
'Tis no such matter. Then you do not love me?

BEATRICE
No truly, but in friendly recompense.

LEONATO
Come, cousin, I am sure you love the gentleman.

CLAUDIO
And I'll be sworn upon't that he loves her,   85
For here's a paper written in his hand,
A halting sonnet of his own pure brain
Fashion'd to Beatrice.

HERO   And here's another,
Writ in my cousin's hand, stolen from her pocket,
Containing her affection unto Benedick.   90

BENEDICK
A miracle! Here's our own hands against our
hearts. Come, I will have thee, but by this light I take
thee for pity.

BEATRICE
I would not deny you, but by this good day I
yield upon great persuasion – and partly to save your   95
life, for I was told you were in a consumption.

LEONATO
Peace! [*to Beatrice*] I will stop your mouth.
[*Hands her to Benedick.*]

'Tis . . . matter – *Not at all*

friendly recompense – *returning friendship to you in kind*

Metre – 12 syl. line

halting – *metrically irregular/limping*, of his own pure brain – *entirely of his own invention*
Be-a-**trice** (equiv. 3 syl.)

pocket – *a bag, not part of the clothing*   stolen (equiv. 1 syl.)
Metre – 12 syl. line

Scene moves into PROSE.
against – *in opposition to what they have professed/witnessing to*
by this light – *(everybody's focus on it being morning contrasts with the many night scenes)*

yield . . . persuasion – *give in because of pressure*
consumption – *wasting away*

SP LEONATO – this line is often reassigned to Benedick, but this is not necessary

DON PEDRO

How dost thou, Benedick, the married man?

BENEDICK

I'll tell thee what, Prince; a college of wit-
crackers cannot flout me out of my humour. Dost thou   100
think I care for a satire or an epigram? No, if a man will
be beaten with brains, 'a shall wear nothing handsome
about him. In brief, since I do purpose to marry, I will
think nothing to any purpose that the world can say
against it; and therefore never flout at me for what I   105
have said against it. For man is a giddy thing, and this
is my conclusion. For thy part, Claudio, I did think
to have beaten thee, but in that thou art like to be my
kinsman, live unbruised and love my cousin.

CLAUDIO

I had well hoped thou wouldst have denied   110
Beatrice, that I might have cudgelled thee out of thy
single life, to make thee a double-dealer – which out
of question thou wilt be, if my cousin do not look
exceeding narrowly to thee.

BENEDICK

Come, come, we are friends. Let's have a   115
dance ere we are married, that we may lighten our own
hearts and our wives' heels.

LEONATO

We'll have dancing afterward.

BENEDICK

First, of my word! Therefore play, music!

college of wit-crackers – *fellowship of jokers*
flout – *goad*
a satire or an epigram – *a verbal jest mocking him*
beaten with brains – *hurt by jibes;* 'a – *he*
'a . . . him – *he would never even dress finely (for fear of presenting a target to satirical wits)*

my conclusion – *what he has decided/how he has ended up*
art like – *are likely*

denied – *refused*
cudgelled – *beaten*
double dealer – *part of a couple/a cheating spouse/apostate to what he claimed previously*
look exceedingly narrowly to thee – *watch you closely*

ere – *before (a reversal of custom)*
heels – *(light-heeled wives are likely to stray)*

of – *by*

Prince, thou art sad – get thee a wife, get thee a wife!   120
There is no staff more reverend than one tipped with
horn.

Enter Messenger.

MESSENGER
My lord, your brother John is ta'en in flight
And brought with armèd men back to Messina.

BENEDICK
Think not on him till tomorrow; I'll devise   125
thee brave punishments for him. Strike up, pipers!

Dance. [Exeunt.]

FINIS

staff – *rod carried as symbol of authority;* tipped with horn – *capped with ivory*

horn – *(the cuckoldry jokes continue until the last possible moment)*

The MESSENGER speaks in VERSE.

ta'en – *taken*

brave – *fearsome*